W9-AMW-310

Record your class number here.

4744

National Restaurant Association
EDUCATIONAL FOUNDATION

175 West Jackson Boulevard, Suite 1500
Chicago, IL 60604-2814
www.nraef.org

ServSafe®

ESSENTIALS | Fourth Edition

National Restaurant Association
EDUCATIONAL FOUNDATION

DISCLAIMER

Essentials without Exam—ES4
ISBN 13: 978-1-58280-180-3
Essentials with Exam—ESX4
ISBN 13: 978-1-58280-179-7
Essentials with Online Exam Voucher—ESV4
ISBN 13: 978-1-58280-188-9
Wiley Essentials without Exam—ES4-W
ISBN 13: 978-0-471-77573-7
Wiley Essentials with Exam—ESX4-W
ISBN 13: 978-0-471-77567-6
Wiley Essentials with Online Exam Voucher—ESV4-W
ISBN 13: 978-0-471-77571-3

Printed in the U.S.A.

10 9 8 7 6

TABLE OF CONTENTS

Introduction

Unit 1   The Sanitation Challenge

A MESSAGE FROM

The National Restaurant Association Educational Foundation

The NRAEF is pleased to bring you the fourth edition of *ServSafe® Essentials*.

By opening this ServSafe book, you are taking the first step in your commitment to food safety. The information in this book will help you apply critical food safety practices to every meal you serve. You can feel good knowing that the ServSafe program was created by the foodservice industry, for the foodservice industry, and leads the way in setting high food safety standards.

In fact, ServSafe training and certification is recognized by more federal, state, and local jurisdictions than any other food safety certification.

Use this book to:

■ **Learn Food Safety Principles.** *ServSafe Essentials* provides critical food safety knowledge that will help you implement and maintain safe foodhandling practices in your establishment.

■ **Teach Your Team Members.** The new **"Take It Back"** reference guides at the end of each section will help you bring essential food safety knowledge back to your employees. Visit *www.ServSafe.com/FoodSafety/resource* for more information.

■ **Sharpen Your Training Skills.** The information presented in the **Employee Food Safety Training section** will help you enhance your skills as a trainer. The training concepts in this section demonstrate different ways to convey essential food safety information to your employees.

■ **Highlight Differences for Your Jurisdiction.** The new **"How This Relates to Me"** areas located throughout the text will help you note differences between the information presented in *ServSafe Essentials* and your jurisdictional requirements.

■ **Evaluate Your Current Food Safety Practices.** The **Food Safety Evaluation Checklist,** located in the Appendix, will help you identify gaps between your current practices and those practices critical to keeping food safe in your operation.

For more information on the NRAEF and its programs, visit *www.nraef.org* or *www.ServSafe.com.*

National Restaurant Association Educational Foundation
The NRAEF is a not-for-profit organization dedicated to fulfilling the educational mission of the National Restaurant Association. As the nation's largest private sector employer, the restaurant and foodservice industry is the cornerstone of the American economy, of career-and-employment opportunities, and of local communities. Focusing on three key strategies of risk management, recruitment, and retention, the NRAEF is the premier provider of educational resources, materials, and programs, which address attracting, developing and retaining the industry's workforce. Sales from all NRAEF products and services benefit the industry by directly supporting the NRAEF's educational initiatives.

The National Restaurant Association Educational Foundation's

INTERNATIONAL FOOD SAFETY COUNCIL®

The International Food Safety Council's mission is to heighten the awareness of the importance of food safety education throughout the restaurant and foodservice industry. The council envisions a future in which foodborne illness no longer exists.

Initiatives

The NRAEF encourages restaurant and foodservice professionals to become involved by participating in council activities such as:

- Food Safety Event—Washington, D.C.

- National Food Safety Education Month®—September, visit *www.nraef.org/nfsem*

For more information about the NRAEF's International Food Safety Council, sponsorship opportunities, and initiatives, please call 312.261.5336, or visit the NRAEF's Web site at *www.nraef.org/ifsc.*

Founding Sponsors

American Egg Board

The Beef Checkoff

Ecolab Inc.

FoodHandler Inc.

SYSCO Corporation

Tyson Foods, Inc.

Campaign Sponsors

Cintas Corporation

Rubbermaid Commercial Products

Past Founding Sponsors

Heinz North America

San Jamar/Katch All

UBF Foodsolutions North America

Acknowledgements

The development of the *ServSafe Essentials* text would not have been possible without the expertise of our many advisors and manuscript reviewers. The NRAEF is pleased to thank the following organizations for their time, effort, and dedication to creating this fourth edition.

American Egg Board

Applebee's International, Inc.

The Beef Checkoff

Black Angus Steakhouse

Buffalo Wild Wings Grill & Bar

Burger King Corporation

Cargill, Inc.

Carlson Restaurants Worldwide, Inc.

Ecolab Inc.

Enrico's Italian Dining

FoodHandler Inc., Safety Management Services

Food Allergy and Anaphylaxis Network

Jack in the Box, Inc.

Jesse Brown Veterans Affairs Medical Center

National Restaurant Association

North American Meat Processors Association

Sodexho, Inc.

SYSCO Corporation

Taylor Farms, Inc.

United Fresh Fruit and Vegetable Association

Walt Disney World Co.

HOW TO USE *SERVSAFE ESSENTIALS*

The plan below will help you study and retain the food safety principles in this textbook that are vital to keeping your establishment safe.

Beginning Each Section

Before you begin reading each section, you can prepare by:

- **Reviewing the learning objectives.** Located on the front page of each section, the learning objectives identify tasks you should be able to do after finishing the section. They are linked to the essential practices for keeping your establishment safe.

- **Completing the Test Your Food Safety Knowledge questions.** Five True or False questions at the beginning of each section will test your prior food safety knowledge. The questions include page references for you to explore the topics further. Answers are located at the back of the section.

Throughout Each Section

Use the following learning tools to help you identify and reinforce the key principles as you read each section:

- **Concepts.** These topics are important for a thorough understanding of food safety. They are identified before the introduction to each section.

- **Exhibits.** These are placed throughout each section to visually reinforce the key principles presented in the text. They include charts, photographs, illustrations, and tables.

- **Icons.** Two types of icons appear in *ServSafe Essentials.*

  - In Sections 5 through 10, an icon representing the various points in the flow of food appears in the left margin. As you read through these sections, you will notice the highlighted portion of the icon changes according to the point within the flow of food being discussed.

Unit 1

The Sanitation Challenge

Apply Your Knowledge

Answers

Page	Activity

1-2 Test Your Food Safety Knowledge

1. True 2. True 3. False 4. True 5. False

1-10 Potentially Hazardous or Not?

1. No	4. Yes	7. No	10. Yes	13. Yes
2. Yes	5. No	8. No	11. No	14. Yes
3. Yes	6. No	9. No	12. Yes	15. No

1-12 Multiple-Choice Study Questions

1. B 2. B 3. B 4. B 5. D

Take It Back*

The following food safety concepts from this section should be taught to your employees:

- Potentially hazardous food
- How food becomes unsafe

The tools below can be used to teach these concepts in fifteen minutes or less using the directions below. Each tool includes content and language appropriate for employees. Choose the tool or tools that work best.

Tool #1:	**Tool #2:**	**Tool #3:**	**Tool #4:**
ServSafe Video 2: *Overview of Foodborne Microorganisms and Allergens*	*ServSafe Employee Guide*	ServSafe Posters and Quiz Sheets	ServSafe Fact Sheets and Optional Activities

Potentially Hazardous Food

Video segment on food supporting growth of microorganisms	**Section 1**		
1 Show employees the segment.	**What a Foodborne Illness Is**		
2 Ask employees to identify food items that are potentially hazardous.	Discuss with employees food items that are potentially hazardous.		

* **Visit the Food Safety Resource Center at *www.ServSafe.com/FoodSafety/resource* to download free posters, quiz sheets, fact sheets, and optional activities and to learn how to obtain *Employee Guides* and videos/DVDs.**

Take It Back*

Tool #1:	Tool #2:	Tool #3:	Tool #4:
ServSafe Video 1: *Introduction to Food Safety*	*ServSafe Employee Guide*	ServSafe Posters and Quiz Sheets	ServSafe Fact Sheets and Optional Activities

How Food Becomes Unsafe

Video segment on how food becomes unsafe

1 Show employees the segment.

2 Ask employees to identify the factors that can cause food to become unsafe.

Section 1

How Food Can Become Unsafe

1 Discuss with employees the factors that can cause food to become unsafe.

2 Complete the Multiple Choice Questions.

Poster: How Food Can Become Unsafe

1 Discuss with employees the factors that can cause food to become unsafe as presented in the poster.

2 Have employees complete the Quiz Sheet: How Food Can Become Unsafe.

* Visit the Food Safety Resource Center at *www.ServSafe.com/FoodSafety/resource* to download free posters, quiz sheets, fact sheets, and optional activities and to learn how to obtain *Employee Guides* and videos/DVDs.

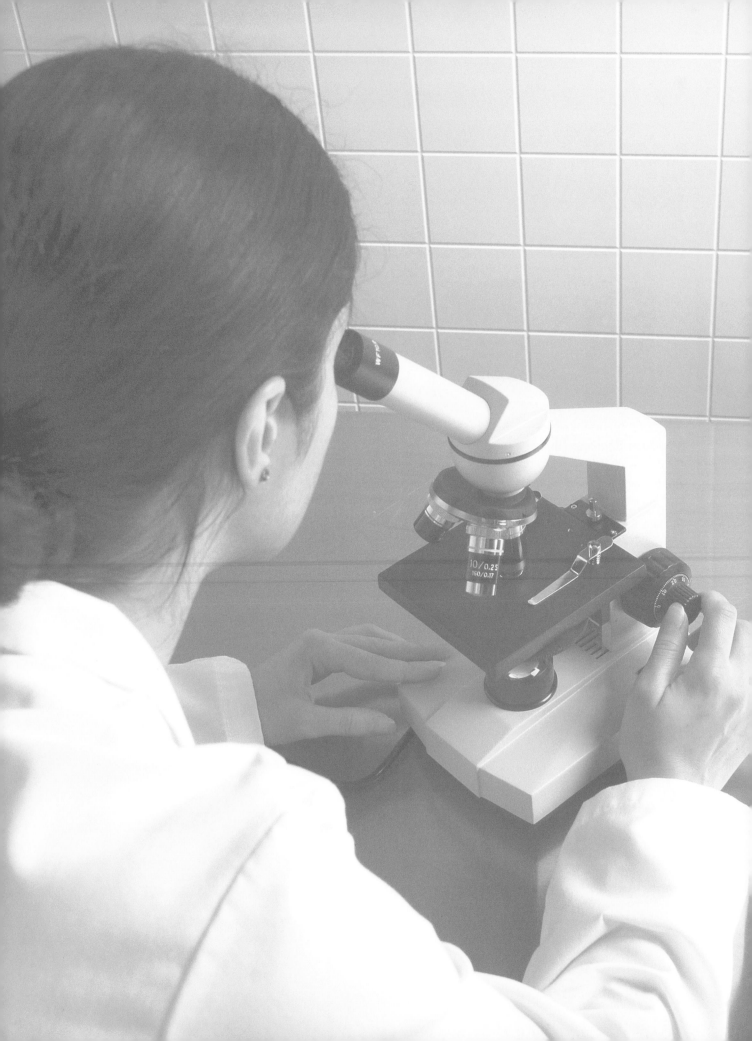

The Microworld

Inside this section:

- Microbial Contaminants
- Classifying Foodborne Illness
- Bacteria
- Viruses
- Parasites
- Fungi

After completing this section, you should be able to:

- Identify factors that affect the growth of foodborne pathogens (FAT TOM).
- Identify major foodborne illnesses and their symptoms.
- Identify characteristics of major foodborne pathogens including sources, food involved in outbreaks, and methods of prevention.
- Differentiate between foodborne infections, intoxications, and toxin-mediated infections.

Apply Your Knowledge	Test Your Food Safety Knowledge

Check to see how much you know about the concepts in this section. Use the page references provided with each question to explore the topic.

1. **True or False:** *Bacillus cereus* is commonly associated with cereal crops, such as rice. *(See page 2-17.)*

2. **True or False:** A foodborne intoxication results when a person eats food containing pathogens, which then grow in the intestines and cause illness. *(See page 2-7.)*

3. **True or False:** Cooking food to the required minimum internal temperature can help prevent listeriosis. *(See page 2-14.)*

4. **True or False:** A person with shigellosis may experience bloody diarrhea. *(See page 2-13.)*

5. **True or False:** Highly acidic food typically does not support the growth of foodborne microorganisms. *(See page 2-5.)*

For answers, please turn to page 2-39.

CONCEPTS

- **Microorganism:** Small, living organism that can only be seen with the aid of a microscope. There are four types of microorganisms that can contaminate food and cause foodborne illness: bacteria, viruses, parasites, and fungi.

- **Pathogens:** Illness-causing microorganisms.

- **Bacteria:** Single-celled living microorganisms that can spoil food and cause foodborne illness. Bacteria present in food can quickly multiply to dangerous levels when food is improperly cooked, held, cooled, and reheated. Some bacteria form spores that can survive cooking temperatures.

- **Virus:** The smallest of the microbial food contaminants. Viruses rely on a living host to reproduce. They usually contaminate food through a foodhandler's improper personal hygiene. Some viruses can survive freezing and cooking temperatures.

- **Parasite:** Microorganism that needs to live in a host organism to survive. Parasites can be found in water and inside many animals, such as cows, chickens, pigs, and fish. Proper cooking and freezing will kill parasites. Avoiding cross-contamination and practicing proper handwashing can also prevent illness.

- **Fungi:** Fungi range in size from microscopic, single-celled organisms to very large, multicellular organisms. Fungi most often cause food to spoil. Mold, yeast, and mushrooms are examples.

- **pH:** Measure of a food's acidity or alkalinity. The pH scale ranges from 0.0 to 14.0. A pH between 7.1 and 14.0 is alkaline, while a pH between 0.0 and 6.9 is acidic. A pH of 7.0 is neutral. Foodborne microorganisms grow well in food that has a neutral to slightly acidic pH (7.5 to 4.6).

- **Spore:** Form that some bacteria can take to protect themselves when nutrients are not available. Spores are commonly found in soil and can contaminate food grown there. A spore can resist heat allowing it to survive cooking temperatures. Spores can also revert back to a form capable of growth. This can occur when food is not held at the proper temperature or cooled or reheated properly.

- **FAT TOM:** Acronym for the conditions needed by foodborne microorganisms to grow: food, acidity, temperature, time, oxygen, and moisture.

- **Temperature danger zone:** The temperature range between 41°F and 135°F (5°C and 57°C) within which foodborne microorganisms grow.

- **Water activity:** Amount of moisture available in food for microorganisms to grow. It is measured on a scale from 0.0 to 1.0, with water having a water activity (a_w) of 1.0. Potentially hazardous food typically has a water activity value of .85 or higher.

- **Mold:** Type of fungus that causes food spoilage. Some molds produce toxins that can cause foodborne illness.

- **Yeast:** Type of fungus that causes food spoilage.

■ **Foodborne infection:** Result of a person eating food containing pathogens, which then grow in the intestines and cause illness. Typically, symptoms of a foodborne infection do not appear immediately.

■ **Foodborne intoxication:** Result of a person eating food containing toxins (poisons) that cause an illness. The toxins may have been produced by pathogens found on the food or may be the result of a chemical contamination. The toxins might also be a natural part of the plant or animal consumed. Typically, symptoms of foodborne intoxication appear quickly, within a few hours.

■ **Foodborne toxin-mediated infection:** Result of a person eating food containing pathogens, which then produce illness-causing toxins in the intestines.

INTRODUCTION

In this section, you will learn about the microorganisms that cause foodborne illness and the conditions that allow them to grow. Understanding these conditions is the first step toward preventing foodborne-illness outbreaks in your establishment.

Microorganisms are small, living organisms that can only be seen with a microscope. While not all microorganisms cause illness, some do. These are called pathogens. Eating food contaminated with foodborne pathogens, or their toxins, is the leading cause of foodborne illness.

MICROBIAL CONTAMINANTS

There are four types of microorganisms that can contaminate food and cause foodborne illness: bacteria, viruses, parasites, and fungi. These microorganisms can also be divided into two groups: spoilage microorganisms and pathogens. Mold is a spoilage microorganism. While its appearance, smell, and taste is not very appetizing, it typically does not cause illness. Pathogens, like *Salmonella* spp. and the hepatitis A virus, can cause some form of illness when ingested. Unlike spoilage microorganisms, pathogens cannot be seen, smelled, or tasted in food.

What Microorganisms Need to Grow: FAT TOM

The six conditions that support the growth of foodborne microorganisms—with the exception of viruses—can be remembered by the acronym FAT TOM. (See *Exhibit 2a.*) A brief explanation of each condition follows.

Exhibit 2a

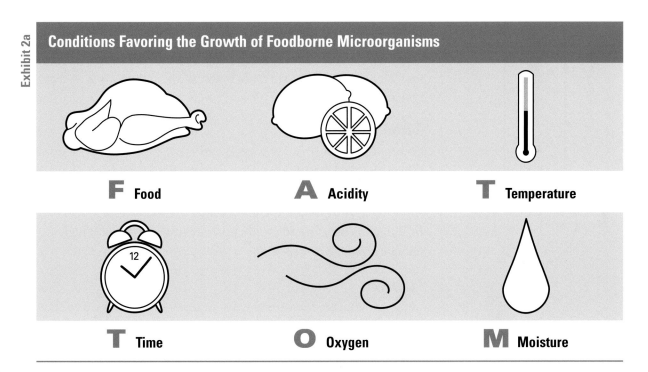

Conditions Favoring the Growth of Foodborne Microorganisms

F Food   **A** Acidity   **T** Temperature

T Time   **O** Oxygen   **M** Moisture

Food

Foodborne microorganisms need nutrients to grow—specifically carbohydrates and proteins. These are commonly found in potentially hazardous food, such as meat, poultry, dairy products, and eggs.

Acidity

pH is a measurement of how acidic or alkaline a food is. The pH scale ranges from 0.0 to 14.0. Food with a pH between 0.0 and 6.9 is acidic, while food with a pH between 7.1 and 14.0 is alkaline. A pH of 7.0 is neutral. Foodborne microorganisms typically do not grow in alkaline foods, such as crackers, or highly acidic foods, such as lemons. They grow best in food that has a neutral or slightly acidic pH (7.5 to 4.6). Unfortunately, the pH of most food falls into this range.

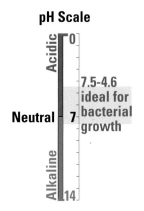

pH Scale

Acidic

0

7.5-4.6 ideal for bacterial growth

Neutral 7

Alkaline

14

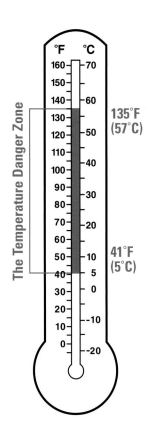

Temperature

Foodborne microorganisms grow well between the temperatures of 41°F and 135°F (5°C and 57°C). This range is known as the temperature danger zone. Exposing microorganisms to temperatures outside the temperature danger zone does not necessarily kill them. Refrigeration temperatures, for example, may only slow their growth. Some bacteria actually grow at refrigeration temperatures.

Food must be handled very carefully when it is thawed, cooked, cooled, and reheated, as it is exposed to the temperature danger zone during these times.

Time

Foodborne microorganisms need sufficient time to grow. Given the right conditions, they are capable of doubling their population every twenty minutes. If potentially hazardous food remains in the temperature danger zone for four hours or longer, foodborne microorganisms can grow to levels high enough to make someone ill.

Oxygen

Some foodborne microorganisms require oxygen to grow while others grow when oxygen is absent. Cooked rice, untreated garlic-and-oil mixtures, and baked potatoes have been associated with certain types of bacteria that grow without oxygen.

Moisture

Most foodborne microorganisms require moisture to grow. The amount of moisture available in food for this growth is called its water activity (a_w). It is measured on a scale from 0.0 to 1.0, with water having a value of 1.0. Potentially hazardous food typically has a water activity value of .85 or higher.

Controlling the Growth of Microorganisms

FAT TOM is the key to controlling microorganisms. Denying any one of these conditions for growth can help keep food safe.

Food processors use several methods to keep microorganisms from growing. This includes:

■ Adding lactic or citric acid to food to make it more acidic

Infection

Illness: Campylobacteriosis *(CAMP-ee-lo-BAK-teer-ee-O-sis)*

Bacteria: *Campylobacter jejuni*
(CAMP-ee-lo-BAK-ter jay-JUNE-ee)

Though *Campylobacter jejuni* is commonly associated with poultry, it has been known to contaminate water. Illness often occurs when poultry is improperly cooked and when raw poultry has been allowed to cross-contaminate other food and food-contact surfaces. Campylobacteriosis is best controlled through proper cooking and the prevention of cross-contamination.

Food Commonly Associated with the Bacteria

- Poultry
- Water contaminated with the bacteria

Most Common Symptoms

- Diarrhea (may be watery or bloody)
- Abdominal cramps
- Fever
- Headache

Most Important Prevention Measures

To reduce the bacteria in food:
- Cook food, particularly poultry, to required minimum internal temperatures.

To prevent the transfer of the bacteria to food:
- Prevent cross-contamination between raw poultry and ready-to-eat food.

Infection

Illness: Salmonellosis *(SAL-men-uh-LO-sis)*

Bacteria: *Salmonella* spp.
(SAL-ma-NEL-uh)

Many farm animals naturally carry *salmonella* spp. It is often associated with poultry and eggs, dairy products, and beef. It has also been found in ready-to-eat food, such as produce that has come in contact with these animals or their waste. Since illness can occur after consuming only a small amount of this type of bacteria, it is critical to cook food properly and to prevent cross-contamination.

Food Commonly Associated with the Bacteria

- Poultry and eggs
- Dairy products
- Beef

Most Common Symptoms

- Diarrhea
- Abdominal cramps
- Vomiting
- Fever

The severity of these symptoms depends upon the health of the person and the amount of bacteria consumed.

Salmonella spp. is often present in a person's feces for several weeks after symptoms have ended.

Most Important Prevention Measures

To reduce the bacteria in food:
- Cook raw beef, poultry, and eggs to required minimum internal temperatures.

To prevent the transfer of the bacteria to food:
- Minimize cross-contamination between raw meat and poultry and ready-to-eat food.
- Exclude foodhandlers from working in the establishment if they have been diagnosed with salmonellosis.

Intoxication

Illness: *Bacillus cereus* Gastroenteritis
(ba-CIL-us SEER-ee-us GAS-tro-EN-ter-I-tiss)

Bacteria: *Bacillus cereus*
(ba-CIL-us SEER-ee-us)

Bacillus cereus is a spore forming bacteria found in soil. It is commonly associated with plants and cereal crops, such as rice. This type of bacteria can produce two different toxins when allowed to grow to high levels. Each causes a different type of illness. Inside food, the bacteria produce an *emetic toxin;* while inside the human intestine, the bacteria create a *diarrheal toxin.* Preventing these illnesses is dependent upon preventing bacterial growth and toxin production. This can be accomplished by cooking, holding, and cooling food properly.

Food Commonly Associated with the Bacteria

Diarrheal toxin:
- Cooked corn
- Cooked potatoes
- Cooked vegetables
- Meat products

Emetic toxin:
- Cooked rice dishes including:
  - Fried rice
  - Rice pudding

Most Common Symptoms

Diarrheal toxin:
- Watery diarrhea
- Abdominal cramps and pain
- Vomiting is absent

Emetic toxin:
- Nausea
- Vomiting

Most Important Prevention Measures

To reduce the bacteria in food:
- Cook food to required minimum internal temperatures.

To prevent the growth of the bacteria in food:
- Hold food at the proper temperature.
- Cool food properly.

Intoxication

Illness: Staphylococcal Gastroenteritis
(STAF-ul-lo-KOK-al GAS-tro-EN-ter-I-tiss)

Bacteria: *Staphylococcus aureus*
(STAF-uh-lo-KOK-us OR-ee-us)

Staphylococcus aureus is primarily found in humans—particularly in the hair, nose, throat, and sores. It is often transferred to food when people carrying this type of bacteria touch these areas and handle food without washing their hands. If allowed to grow to large numbers in food, the bacteria can produce toxins that cause the illness when eaten. Since cooking cannot destroy these toxins, it is critical to prevent bacterial growth. Practicing good personal hygiene can prevent the transfer of the bacteria to food.

Food Commonly Associated with the Bacteria

Food that requires handling during preparation including:

- Salads containing potentially hazardous food (egg, tuna, chicken, macaroni)
- Deli meats

Most Common Symptoms

- Nausea
- Vomiting and retching
- Abdominal cramps

Most Important Prevention Measures

To prevent the transfer of the bacteria to food:

- Wash hands when necessary, especially after touching the hair, face, or body.
- Properly cover cuts on hands and arms.
- Restrict foodhandlers with infected cuts on hands or arms from working with or around food and food equipment.

To prevent the growth of the bacteria in food:

- Minimize the time food spends in the temperature danger zone.
  - Cook, hold, and cool food properly.

Intoxication

Illness: Botulism *(BOT-chew-liz-um)*

Bacteria: *Clostridium botulinum*
(klos-TRID-ee-um BOT-chew-line-um)

While *Clostridium botulinum* forms spores that can be found in almost any food, it is commonly associated with produce grown in the soil, such as onions, potatoes, and carrots. This type of bacteria does not grow well in refrigerated or highly acidic food, nor in food with low water activity. However, it does grow without oxygen and can produce a deadly toxin when food is temperature abused. Without treatment, death is likely. Holding, cooling, and reheating food properly inhibits the growth of the bacteria and reduces the potential for illness.

Food Commonly Associated with the Bacteria

- Improperly canned food
- Reduced-oxygen-packaged (ROP) food
- Temperature-abused vegetables such as:
  - Baked potatoes
  - Untreated garlic-and-oil mixtures

Most Common Symptoms

Initially:
- Nausea and vomiting

Later:
- Weakness
- Double vision
- Difficulty speaking and swallowing

Most Important Prevention Measures

- Hold, cool, and reheat food properly.
- Inspect canned food for damage.

Toxin-Mediated Infection

Illness: *Clostridium perfringens* Gastroenteritis
(klos-TRID-ee-um per-FRIN-jins GAS-tro-EN-ter-I-tiss)

Bacteria: *Clostridium perfringens*
(klos-TRID-ee-um per-FRIN-jins)

Clostridium perfringens is found naturally in soil where it forms spores that allow it to survive. It is also carried in the intestines of both animals and humans. People become ill after eating this type of bacteria, which produces toxins once inside their intestines. While *Clostridium perfringens* does not grow at refrigeration temperatures, it grows *very rapidly* in food in the temperature danger zone. To prevent illness, it is critical to keep the bacteria from growing, especially when holding, cooling, and reheating food.

Food Commonly Associated with the Bacteria

- Meat
- Poultry
- Dishes made with meat and poultry, such as:
  - Stews
  - Gravies

Commercially prepared food is not often involved in outbreaks.

Most Common Symptoms

- Diarrhea
- Severe abdominal pain

Nausea is uncommon and fever and vomiting are absent.

Most Important Prevention Measures

To prevent the growth of the bacteria (especially in meat dishes):
- Cool and reheat food properly.
- Hold food at the proper temperature.

Infection

Illness: Hepatitis A *(HEP-a-TI-tiss)*

Virus: Hepatitis A *(HEP-a-TI-tiss)*

Hepatitis A is primarily found in the feces of people infected with the virus. While water and many types of food can become contaminated, the virus is more commonly associated with ready-to-eat food items. It has also been found in shellfish contaminated by sewage. Hepatitis A is often transferred to food when infected foodhandlers touch food or equipment with fingers containing feces. It is only necessary to consume a small amount of the virus to become ill. Proper handwashing is critical to preventing the illness, since cooking does not destroy the hepatitis A virus.

Food Commonly Associated with the Virus

- Ready-to-eat food, including:
  - Deli meats
  - Produce
  - Salads
- Raw and partially cooked shellfish

Most Common Symptoms

Initially:
- Fever (mild)
- General weakness
- Nausea
- Abdominal pain

Later:
- Jaundice

An infected person may not show symptoms for weeks, but can be very infectious.

Most Important Prevention Measures

To prevent the transfer of the virus to food:
- Wash hands properly.
- Exclude employees from the establishment who have jaundice or have been diagnosed with hepatitis A.
- Minimize bare-hand contact with ready-to-eat food.

Other prevention measures:
- Purchase shellfish from approved, reputable suppliers.
- Inform high-risk populations to consult a physician before regularly consuming raw or partially cooked shellfish.

Infection

Illness: Norovirus Gastroenteritis *(NOR-o-VI-rus GAS-tro-EN-ter-I-tiss)*

Virus: Norovirus *(NOR-o-VI-rus)*

Norovirus is primarily found in the feces of people infected with the virus. It has also been found in contaminated water. Like hepatitis A, it is commonly associated with ready-to-eat food. The virus is very contagious and is often transferred to food when infected foodhandlers touch the food with fingers containing feces. Consuming even a small amount of the virus can lead to infection. People become contagious within a few hours of eating contaminated food. Proper handwashing is essential to prevent the illness. It is also critical to prevent foodhandlers from working with food if they have symptoms related to the illness.

Food Commonly Associated with the Virus

- Ready-to-eat food
- Shellfish contaminated by sewage

Most Common Symptoms

- Vomiting
- Diarrhea
- Nausea
- Abdominal cramps

Norovirus is often present in a person's feces for days after symptoms have ended.

Most Important Prevention Measures

To prevent the transfer of the virus to food:
- Exclude foodhandlers with diarrhea and vomiting from the establishment.
- Exclude employees who have been diagnosed with norovirus from the establishment.
- Wash hands properly.

Other prevention measures:
- Purchase shellfish from approved, reputable suppliers.

PARASITES

Parasites are living organisms that need a host to survive. They infect many animals—such as cows, chicken, pigs, and fish—and can be transmitted to humans. Parasites are larger than bacteria, but are still very small—often microscopic. They are a hazard to both food and water.

Major Foodborne Illnesses Caused by Parasites

There are four major foodborne illnesses caused by parasites. They are all classified as infections. For each illness, it is important to understand its common source; the food commonly associated with it; its most common symptoms; and the most important measures that can be taken to prevent the illness from occurring. The table on the following page provides a high-level overview of these characteristics. While not all-inclusive, this information will help you see the similarities and differences that will make it easier to remember each illness.

Parasitic Foodborne Illnesses

Major Foodborne Illnesses Caused by Parasites

Illness Characteristics	Type of Illness				Intoxication	Toxin-Mediated Infection
	Infection					
	Anisakiasis	Cyclosporiasis	Cryptosporidiosis	Giardiasis		
Commonly Associated Food						
Poultry						
Eggs						
Meat						
Fish	x					
Shellfish	x					
Ready-to-eat food						
Produce		x	x			
Cereal crops						
Dairy						
Contaminated water		x	x	x		
Most Common Symptoms						
Diarrhea	x	x	x			
Abdominal pain/cramps	x	x	x	x		
Nausea	x	x	x	x		
Vomiting	x					
Fever		x		x		
Headache						
Most Important Prevention Measures						
Proper handwashing		x	x	x		
Proper cooking	x					
Proper holding						
Proper cooling						
Proper reheating						
Approved suppliers	x	x	x			
Exclude foodhandlers		x	x	x		
Prevent cross-contamination	x					

Infection

Illness: Anisakiasis *(ANN-ih-SAHK-ee-AH-sis)*

Parasite: *Anisakis simplex*
(ANN-ih-SAHK-iss SIM-plex)

Anisakis simplex is a worm-like parasite found in certain fish and shellfish. An illness can develop when raw or undercooked seafood containing the parasite is eaten. It can be either invasive or noninvasive. In its noninvasive form, the person coughs the parasite from the body. In the invasive form, the parasite penetrates the lining of the stomach or small intestine and must be surgically removed. To prevent illness, it is critical to cook seafood properly. It is important to purchase seafood from an approved, reputable supplier.

Food Commonly Associated with the Parasite

Raw and undercooked:
- Herring
- Cod
- Halibut
- Mackerel
- Pacific salmon

Most Common Symptoms

Non-invasive:
- Tingling in throat
- Coughing up worms

Invasive:
- Stomach pain
- Nausea
- Vomiting
- Diarrhea

Most Important Prevention Measures

- Cook fish to required minimum internal temperatures.
- Purchase fish from approved, reputable suppliers.

If fish will be served raw or undercooked:
- Purchase sushi-grade fish.
- Ensure sushi-grade fish has been frozen by the supplier to the proper time-temperature requirements.

Infection

Illness: Cyclosporiasis *(SI-klo-spor-I-uh-sis)*

Parasite:
Cyclospora cayetanensis
(SI-klo-SPOR-uh KI-uh-te-NEN-sis)

Cyclospora cayetanensis is a parasite that has been found in contaminated water and has been associated with produce irrigated or washed with contaminated water. It can also be found in the feces of people infected with the parasite. Foodhandlers can transfer the parasite to food when they touch it with fingers containing feces. For this reason, foodhandlers with diarrhea must be excluded from the establishment. It is also critical to purchase produce from an approved, reputable supplier.

Food Commonly Associated with the Parasite

- Produce irrigated or washed with water containing the parasite

Most Common Symptoms

- Nausea (mild to severe)
- Abdominal cramping
- Mild fever
- Diarrhea alternating with constipation

Symptoms are more severe in people with weakened immune systems.

Most Important Prevention Measures

- Purchase produce from approved, reputable suppliers.

To prevent the transfer of the parasite to food:
- Exclude foodhandlers with diarrhea from the establishment.
- Wash hands properly to minimize risk of cross-contamination.

Infection

Illness: Cryptosporidiosis *(KRIP-TOH-spor-id-ee-O-sis)*

Parasite:
Cryptosporidium parvum
(KRIP-TOH-spor-ID-ee-um PAR-vum)

Cryptosporidium parvum is a parasite that has been found in contaminated water, produce that has been irrigated with contaminated water, and cows and other herd animals. It can also be found in the feces of people infected with the parasite. Foodhandlers can transfer the parasite to food when they touch it with fingers containing feces. It is common for the parasite to be spread from person to person in day-care and medical communities. For this reason, proper handwashing is essential to prevent the illness. It is also critical to purchase produce from an approved, reputable supplier.

Food Commonly Associated with the Parasite

- Untreated or improperly treated water
- Contaminated produce

Most Common Symptoms

- Watery diarrhea
- Stomach cramps
- Nausea
- Weight loss

Symptoms will be more severe in people with weakened immune systems.

Most Important Prevention Measures

- Purchase produce from approved, reputable suppliers.
- Use properly treated water.

To prevent the transfer of the parasite to food:

- Exclude foodhandlers with diarrhea from the establishment.
- Wash hands properly to minimize the risk of cross-contamination.

Infection

Illness: Giardiasis *(jee-are-dee-AH-sis)*

Parasite: *Giardia duodenalis*
(jee-ARE-dee-uh do-WAH-den-AL-is)
(also known as *G. lamblia,* or *G. intestinalsis*)

Giardia duodenalis is a parasite that has been found in improperly treated water. It can be found in the feces of infected people. Foodhandlers can transfer the parasite to food when they touch it with fingers contaminated with feces. It is common for the parasite to be spread from person to person in day-care centers. For this reason, proper handwashing is essential to prevent the illness. It is also critical to use water that has been properly treated.

Food Commonly Associated with the Parasite

- Improperly treated water

Most Common Symptoms

Initially:	Later:
■ Fever	■ Loose stools
	■ Abdominal cramps
	■ Nausea

Most Important Prevention Measures

- Use properly treated water.

To prevent the transfer of the parasite to food:

- Exclude foodhandlers with diarrhea from the establishment.
- Wash hands properly to minimize risk of cross-contamination.

Apply Your Knowledge

Who Am I? Part 2

Identify the virus or parasite from the characteristics given for each and write its name in the space provided.

1 _____

- I can produce a mild fever and general weakness.
- I am primarily found in the feces of infected people.
- I am more commonly associated with ready-to-eat food items.
- Purchasing shellfish from an approved supplier can be a safeguard against me.

2 _____

- I can produce a fever and loose stool.
- I have been found in improperly treated water.
- Excluding foodhandlers with diarrhea from the establishment can be a safeguard against me.
- I am easily spread in day-care centers.

3 _____

- Cooking seafood can destroy me.
- I have been found in herring.
- Sometimes I produce a tingling in the throat.
- Purchasing seafood from approved suppliers can prevent me.

4 _____

- I am often associated with ready-to-eat food.
- Proper handwashing is essential to prevent me.
- I am primarily found in the feces of people I infect.
- People become contagious within a few hours of eating me.

5 _____

- I cause stomach cramps and weight loss.
- I am found in cows and other herd animals.
- I am commonly spread from person to person.
- Purchasing produce from approved suppliers is critical to prevent me.

For answers, please turn to page 2-39.

FUNGI

Fungi range in size from microscopic, single-celled organisms to very large, multicellular organisms. They are found naturally in air, soil, plants, water, and some food. Mold, yeast, and mushrooms are examples of fungi.

Molds

Molds share some basic characteristics:

- They spoil food and sometimes cause illness.

- They grow under almost any condition but grow well in acidic food with low water activity.

- Freezing temperatures prevent or reduce the growth of molds but do not destroy them.

- Some molds produce toxins such as aflatoxins.

While cooking can destroy mold cells and spores, some toxins can remain. To avoid illness, throw out all moldy food, unless the mold is a natural part of the product (e.g., cheese such as Gorgonzola, Brie, and Camembert). The Food and Drug Administration (FDA) recommends cutting away any moldy areas in hard cheese—at least one inch (2.5 centimeters) around them.

Yeasts

Yeast on Jelly

Food that has been spoiled by yeast should be discarded.

Some yeasts have the ability to spoil food rapidly. Carbon dioxide and alcohol are produced as yeast consumes food. Yeast spoilage may, therefore, produce a smell or taste of alcohol. Yeast may appear as a pink discoloration or slime and may bubble.

Yeasts are similar to molds in that they grow well in acidic food with low water activity, such as jellies, jams, syrup, honey, and fruit juice. Food that has been spoiled by yeast should be discarded. (See *Exhibit 2b.*)

Apply Your Knowledge	A Case in Point

1 Based on the information given, what type of microorganism caused the illness—bacteria, virus, parasite?

2 What is the name of the microorganism most likely responsible for the outbreak?

3 Is this illness an infection, intoxication, or toxin-mediated infection?

A day-care center decided to prepare stir-fried rice to serve for lunch the next day. The rice was cooked to the proper temperature at 1:00 p.m. It was then covered and placed on a countertop, where it was allowed to cool at room temperature. At 6:00 p.m., the cook placed the rice in the refrigerator. At 9:00 a.m. the following day, the rice was combined with the other ingredients for stir-fried rice and cooked to 165°F (74°C) for at least fifteen seconds. The cook covered the rice and left it on the stove until noon when she reheated it. Within an hour of eating the rice, several of the children complained that they were nauseous and began to vomit.

For answers, please turn to page 2-39.

SUMMARY

Microorganisms are responsible for the majority of foodborne illness. Understanding how they grow, contaminate food, and affect humans is critical to understanding how to prevent the foodborne illnesses they cause.

The acronym FAT TOM—which stands for Food, Acidity, Temperature, Time, Oxygen, and Moisture—is the key to controlling the growth of microorganisms.

Foodborne illnesses are classified as infections, intoxications, or toxin-mediated infections. Foodborne infections result when a person eats food containing pathogens, which then grow in the intestines and cause illness. Typically, symptoms do not appear immediately. Foodborne intoxications result when a person eats food containing toxins produced by pathogens found on the food or which are the result of a chemical contamination. The toxins might also be a natural part of a plant or animal consumed. Typically, symptoms of foodborne intoxication appear quickly, within a few hours. Foodborne toxin-mediated infections result when a person eats food that contains pathogens, which then produce illness-causing toxins in the intestines.

Of all foodborne microorganisms, bacteria are of greatest concern to the restaurant and foodservice manager. Under favorable conditions, bacteria can reproduce very rapidly. Although they may be resistant to low, even freezing, temperatures, they can be killed by high temperatures, such as those reached during cooking. Certain bacteria, however, can change into a different form, called spores, to protect themselves. Since spores are commonly found on food grown in or exposed to soil, it is important to hold, cool, and reheat food properly. This will prevent spores that might be present from reverting back to a form capable of growing and causing illness.

Viruses are the smallest of the microbial contaminants. While a virus cannot reproduce in food, once consumed, it will cause illness. Practicing good personal hygiene and minimizing bare-hand contact with ready-to-eat food is an important defense against viral foodborne illnesses.

Parasites are organisms that need to live in a host organism to survive. This includes animals such as cows, chickens, pigs, and fish. Proper cooking and freezing can kill parasites.

Fungi, such as molds and yeasts, are generally responsible for spoiling food. Some molds, however, can produce harmful toxins. For this reason, food containing mold should always be discarded—unless it is a natural part of the product. Yeasts can spoil food rapidly. Food spoiled by yeast should also be discarded.

Apply Your Knowledge

Use these questions to test your knowledge of the concepts presented in this section.

Multiple-Choice Study Questions

1. Foodborne microorganisms grow well at temperatures between
   A. 32°F and 70°F (0°C and 21°C).
   B. 38°F and 155°F (3°C and 68°C).
   C. 41°F and 135°F (5°C and 57°C).
   D. 70°F and 165°F (21°C and 74°C).

2. Which condition does *not* typically support the growth of microorganisms?
   A. Moisture
   B. Protein
   C. Time
   D. High acidity

3. Which microorganism is primarily found in the hair, nose, and throat of humans?
   A. Hepatitis A virus
   B. *Giardia duodenalis*
   C. *Staphylococcus aureus*
   D. *Clostridium botulinum*

4. While commonly associated with ground beef, which microorganism has also been associated with contaminated lettuce?
   A. *Salmonella* spp.
   B. *Campylobacter jejuni*
   C. Shiga toxin-producing *E. coli*
   D. Norovirus

5. A person who has campylobacteriosis may experience
   A. chills and skin lesions.
   B. weakness and double vision.
   C. headache and bloody diarrhea.
   D. diarrhea alternating with constipation.

Continued on the next page...

Apply Your Knowledge   **Multiple-Choice Study Questions** *continued*

6. Which practice can help prevent salmonellosis?

   A. Purchasing sushi-grade fish

   B. Inspecting canned food for damage

   C. Cooking poultry and eggs to the proper temperature

   D. Purchasing oysters from reputable, approved suppliers

7. Which practice can help prevent staphylococcal gastroenteritis?

   A. Prohibiting the use of unpasteurized dairy products

   B. Controlling flies inside and outside the establishment

   C. Purchasing shellfish from reputable, approved sources

   D. Restricting foodhandlers with infected cuts from working around food

8. Which microorganism has been associated with produce irrigated with contaminated water?

   A. *Anisakis simplex*

   B. *Vibrio parahaemolyticus*

   C. *Cyclospora cayetanensis*

   D. *Clostridium perfringens*

9. Which statement about foodborne mold is *not* true?

   A. Some types produce toxins.

   B. It grows well in acidic food.

   C. Freezing temperatures destroy it.

   D. It grows well in food with little moisture.

10. The type of illness that results when a person eats food containing pathogens, which then grow in the intestines and cause illness, is called a

    A. foodborne infection.

    B. foodborne intoxication.

    C. foodborne toxin-mediated infection.

    D. foodborne gastroenteritis.

For answers, please turn to page 2-39.

Apply Your Knowledge

Answers

Page	Activity

2-2   Test Your Food Safety Knowledge
1. True   2. False   3. True   4. True   5. True

2-7   What I Need to Grow!
Correct Answer: 2

2-22   Who Am I? Part 1
1. *Salmonella* spp.
2. *Vibrio vulnificus*
3. *Bacillus cereus*
4. *Clostridium perfringens*
5. *Clostridium botulinum*

2-33   Who Am I? Part 2
1. Hepatitis A virus
2. *Giardia duodenalis*
3. *Anisakis simplex*
4. Norovirus
5. *Cryptosporidium parvum*

2-35   A Case in Point
1. Bacteria
2. *Bacillus cereus* was the microorganism responsible for the outbreak.
3. Given the rapid onset and the symptoms, the illness was most likely an intoxication.

2-37   Multiple-Choice Study Questions

1. C	3. C	5. C	7. D	9. C
2. D	4. C	6. C	8. C	10. A

Take It Back*

The following food safety concept from this section should be taught to your employees:

■ How microorganisms make food unsafe

The tools below can be used to teach these concepts in fifteen minutes or less using the directions below. Each tool includes content and language appropriate for employees. Choose the tool or tools that work best.

Tool #1: ServSafe Video 2: *Overview of Foodborne Microorganisms and Allergens*	**Tool #2:** *ServSafe Employee Guide*	**Tool #3:** ServSafe Posters and Quiz Sheets	**Tool #4:** ServSafe Fact Sheets and Optional Activities

How Microorganisms Make Food Unsafe

Video segment on microbial contaminants	**Section 1** **What a Foodborne Illness Is**		
1 Show employees the segment. **2** Ask employees to identify the four types of microorganisms and explain how bacteria can make food unsafe.	Discuss with employees the four types of microorganisms. Explain how bacteria can make food unsafe.		

* Visit the Food Safety Resource Center at *www.ServSafe.com/FoodSafety/resource* to download free posters, quiz sheets, fact sheets, and optional activities and to learn how to obtain *Employee Guides* and videos/DVDs.

Notes

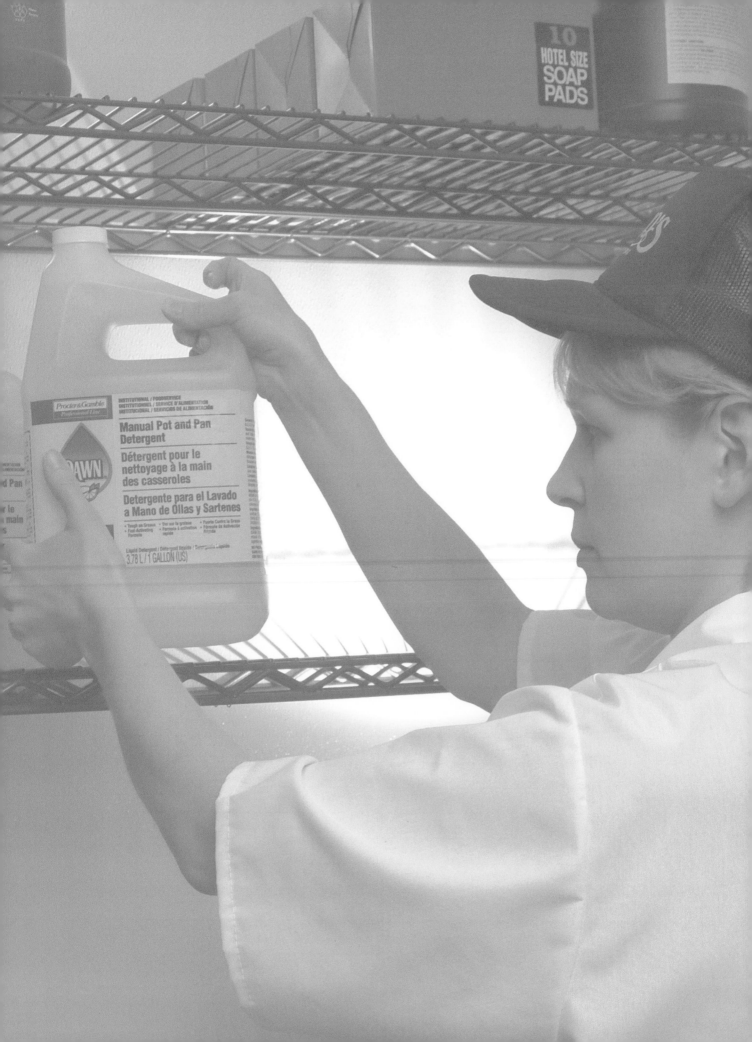

Contamination, Food Allergens, and Foodborne Illness

Inside this section:
- Biological Contamination
- Chemical Contamination
- Physical Contamination
- The Deliberate Contamination of Food
- Food Allergens

After completing this section, you should be able to:
- Identify biological, chemical, and physical contaminants.
- Identify methods to prevent biological, chemical, and physical contamination.
- Identify the eight most common allergens, associated symptoms, and methods of prevention.

Apply Your Knowledge	Test Your Food Safety Knowledge
Check to see how much you know about the concepts in this section. Use the page references provided with each question to explore the topic.	

Test Your Food Safety Knowledge

1. **True or False:** A person with ciguatera fish poisoning often sweats and experiences a burning sensation in the mouth. *(See page 3-7.)*

2. **True or False:** Cooking can destroy the toxins in toxic wild mushrooms. *(See page 3-13.)*

3. **True or False:** Copper utensils and equipment can cause an illness when used to prepare acidic food. *(See page 3-15.)*

4. **True or False:** When transferring a cleaning chemical to a spray bottle, it is unnecessary to label the bottle if the chemical is clearly visible. *(See page 3-15.)*

5. **True or False:** A person with a shellfish allergy who unknowingly eats soup made with clam juice may experience a tightening in the throat. *(See page 3-19.)*

For answers, please turn to page 3-25.

CONCEPTS

- **Biological contaminant:** Microbial contaminant that may cause foodborne illness. These contaminants include bacteria, viruses, parasites, fungi, and biological toxins.

- **Chemical contaminant:** Chemical substance that can cause a foodborne illness. Food can become contaminated by a variety of chemical substances normally found in restaurant and foodservice establishments, including toxic metals, pesticides, cleaning products, sanitizers, and equipment lubricants.

- **Physical contaminant:** Foreign object that is accidentally introduced into food or a naturally occurring object, such as a bone in a fillet, that poses a physical hazard. Common physical contaminants include metal shavings from cans, staples from cartons, glass from broken light bulbs, blades from plastic or rubber scrapers, fingernails, hair, bandages, dirt, and bones.

- **Food security:** Preventing or eliminating the deliberate contamination of food.

- **Biological toxins:** Poisons produced by pathogens and found in some plants and animals. Toxins may be a natural part of the plant or animal or may occur in an animal as a result of diet.

- **Ciguatera fish poisoning:** Illness that occurs when a person eats fish that has consumed ciguatoxin which is found in certain marine algae. The toxin accumulates in fish when they consume smaller fish that have eaten the algae. Ciguatoxin is commonly associated with predatory reef fish such as barracuda, grouper, jacks, and snapper caught in the Pacific Ocean, western Indian Ocean, and the Caribbean Sea.

- **Scombroid poisoning (Histamine poisoning):** Illness caused by consuming high levels of histamine, a toxin that forms when scombroid and other species of fish are subjected to time-temperature abuse. Scombroid fish include tuna, bonito, mackerel, and mahi mahi.

- **Toxic metal poisoning:** Illness that results when food containing toxic metals is eaten. It usually occurs when acidic food is handled with utensils or prepared in equipment containing these metals. It can also occur when carbonated beverage dispensers are improperly installed.

- **Food allergy:** The body's negative reaction to a particular food protein. The most common food allergens include milk and dairy products, eggs and egg products, fish, shellfish, wheat, soy and soy products, peanuts, and tree nuts.

INTRODUCTION

Food is considered contaminated when it contains hazardous substances. These substances may be biological, chemical, or physical. The most common food contaminants are biological contaminants that belong to the microworld—bacteria, parasites, viruses, and fungi. Most foodborne illnesses result from these contaminants, but biological and chemical toxins are also responsible for many foodborne illnesses. While these hazards pose a significant threat to food, the danger from physical hazards should also be recognized.

A thorough understanding of the causes of biological, chemical, and physical contamination will aid in prevention of foodborne illnesses and help you keep food safe.

BIOLOGICAL CONTAMINATION

As you learned in Section 2, foodborne intoxication occurs when a person eats food that contains toxins. The toxin may have been produced by pathogens found in the food or may be the result of a chemical contamination. The toxin could also come from a plant or animal that was eaten.

Toxins in seafood, plants, and mushrooms are responsible for many cases of foodborne illness in the United States each year. Most of these biological toxins are a natural part of the plant or animal. Some occur in animals as a result of their diet.

Fish Toxins

Some fish toxins are systemic—produced by the fish itself. Pufferfish, moray eels, and freshwater minnows all produce systemic toxins. Cooking does not destroy them. Due to the extreme risk posed by pufferfish, it should not be served unless the chef has been licensed to prepare it.

While some fish toxins are systemic, microorganisms on fish produce others. Some occur when predatory fish consume smaller fish that have eaten the toxin.

Major Foodborne Illnesses Caused by Fish Toxins

There are two major foodborne illnesses caused by fish toxins. It is important to understand the most common types of fish associated with each toxin, the most common symptoms, and the most important measures that can be taken to prevent the illness from occurring. The table on the next page provides a high-level overview of these characteristics. While not all-inclusive, this information will help you see the similarities and differences that will make it easier to remember each illness.

In general, purchasing fish from an approved, reputable supplier is the best way to guard against an illness associated with fish toxins. Additionally, check the temperature of fish upon delivery, making sure it has been received at 41°F (5°C) or lower. Refuse product that has been thawed and refrozen, as this is a sign that the fish has been time-temperature abused.

Exhibit 3a

Toxic Metals

Acidic food prepared in equipment made from toxic metals, such as copper, can cause illness.

Toxic Metals

Utensils and equipment that contain toxic metals—such as lead in a pewter pitcher, copper in a saucepan, or zinc in a galvanized bucket—can cause toxic metal poisoning. (See *Exhibit 3a.*) If acidic food is stored in or prepared with this equipment, the toxic metals can be transferred to the food. Only food-grade utensils and equipment should be used to prepare and store food.

Carbonated-beverage dispensers that are improperly installed can also create a hazard. If carbonated water is allowed to flow back into the copper supply lines, it could leach copper from the line and contaminate the beverage. Beverage-dispensing systems should be installed and maintained by professionals who will ensure that a proper backflow-prevention device is installed.

Chemicals and Pesticides

Chemicals such as cleaning products, polishes, lubricants, and sanitizers can contaminate food if they are improperly used or stored. To prevent contamination and keep food safe:

- Follow the directions supplied by the manufacturer when using chemicals.

- Exercise caution when using chemicals during operating hours to prevent contamination of food and food-preparation areas.

- Store chemicals away from food, utensils, and equipment used for food. Keep them in a separate storage area in their original container.

- If chemicals must be transferred to smaller containers or spray bottles, label each container appropriately.

Pesticides are often used to control pests in food preparation and storage areas. They should only be applied by a licensed pest control operator (PCO). All food should be wrapped or stored before pesticides are applied. If pesticides are stored in the establishment, exercise the same care as with other chemicals used there.

See *Exhibit 3b* on the next page for a summary of common chemical contaminants.

Exhibit 3b

Chemical Contaminants		
Source of Contamination	**Associated Food**	**Prevention Measures**
Toxic Metals		
Utensils and equipment containing toxic metals, such as lead, copper, and zinc	■ Any food, but especially high-acid food, such as sauerkraut, tomatoes, and citrus products ■ Carbonated beverages	■ Use only food-grade containers. ■ Use only food-grade brushes on food; do not use paintbrushes or wire brushes. ■ Do not use enamelware, which may chip and expose the underlying metal. ■ Do not use equipment or utensils made of toxic metals. ■ Use a backflow-prevention device on carbonated beverage dispensers.
Chemicals		
Cleaning products, polishes, lubricants, and sanitizers	■ Any food	■ Follow manufacturers' directions for storage and use; use only recommended amounts. ■ Store away from food, utensils, and equipment used for food. ■ Store in original, labeled containers. ■ Utensils used for dispensing chemicals should never be used to handle food. ■ If chemicals must be transferred to smaller containers or spray bottles, label each container appropriately. ■ Use only food-grade lubricants or oils on kitchen equipment or utensils.
Pesticides		
Used in food-preparation and storage areas	■ Any food	■ Pesticides should only be applied by a licensed professional. ■ Wrap or store all food before pesticides are applied.

Apply Your Knowledge	A Case in Point

1 Explain why the mahi-mahi steaks caused an outbreak of scombroid poisoning.

Roberto received a shipment of frozen mahi-mahi steaks. The steaks were frozen solid at the time of delivery, and the packages were sealed and contained a large amount of ice crystals, indicating they had been time-temperature abused. Roberto accepted the mahi-mahi steaks and thawed them in the refrigerator at a temperature of 38°F (3°C). The thawed fish steaks were then held at this temperature during the evening shift and were cooked to order. The chefs followed the appropriate guidelines for preparing, cooking, and serving the fish, monitoring time and temperature throughout the process. Unfortunately, the fish steaks caused several scombroid fish poisonings.

For answers, please turn to page 3-25.

SUMMARY

A foodborne intoxication occurs when a person eats food that contains toxins. The toxin may have been produced by pathogens found on the food or may be the result of a chemical contamination. The toxin could also come from a plant or animal that was eaten.

While some fish toxins are produced by the fish itself, microorganisms on fish are responsible for others—such as histamine produced when scombroid fish are time-temperature abused. Some fish toxins occur as a result of the fish's diet. Ciguatoxin, for example, is found in certain predatory reef fish that have eaten smaller fish, which have consumed the toxin. It is critical to purchase fish from approved, reputable suppliers since these toxins cannot be destroyed by cooking or freezing.

Many toxins associated with shellfish are found in certain types of toxic marine algae. The shellfish become contaminated as they filter the toxic algae from the water. As with fish, purchasing shellfish from approved, reputable suppliers is the most important safeguard against foodborne illness.

Foodborne illnesses associated with mushrooms are almost always caused by the consumption of toxic, wild mushrooms collected by amateur mushroom hunters. For this reason, do not use mushrooms picked in the wild or products made with them unless they have been purchased from approved, reputable suppliers. Plant toxins are another form of biological contamination. In general, toxic plant species and products prepared with them should be avoided.

Chemical contaminants can come from a variety of substances normally found in restaurants and foodservice establishments. These include toxic metals, pesticides, cleaning products, sanitizers, and lubricants. To prevent contamination, only use food-grade utensils and equipment to prepare and store food. Cleaning products, polishes, lubricants, and sanitizers should be used as directed. Exercise caution when using these chemicals during operating hours and store them properly. If used, pesticides should be applied by a licensed professional.

Physical contamination can occur when physical objects are accidentally introduced into food or when naturally occurring objects, such as the bones in fish, pose a physical hazard. Closely inspect the food you receive and take steps to ensure food will not become physically contaminated during its flow through your operation.

Food security addresses the prevention or elimination of the deliberate contamination of food. Contamination can occur in biological, chemical, physical, nuclear, or radioactive form. The key to protecting food is to make it as difficult as possible for tampering to occur. Managers must develop and maintain a food security program that focuses on the potential threats posed by the interior, exterior, and human elements of their establishment.

Many people have food allergies. Managers and employees should be aware of the most common food allergens, which include milk and dairy products, eggs and egg products, fish, shellfish, wheat, soy and soy products, peanuts, and tree nuts. You and your employees should be able to inform customers of these and other potential food allergens that may be included in food served at your establishment.

Apply Your Knowledge

Multiple-Choice Study Questions

Use these questions to test your knowledge of the concepts presented in this section.

1. Fresh tuna steaks have been delivered to your establishment at an internal temperature of 50°F (5°C). You should reject the tuna since serving it could lead to which of these foodborne illnesses?

   A. Anisakiasis

   B. Scombroid poisoning

   C. Ciguatera fish poisoning

   D. *Vibrio vulnificus* gastroenteritis

2. Which is *not* a common food allergen?

   A. Eggs

   B. Dairy products

   C. Peanuts

   D. Pork

3. All of these practices can lead to toxic metal poisoning *except*

   A. cooking tomato sauce in a copper pot.

   B. storing orange juice in a pewter pitcher.

   C. using a backflow-prevention device on a carbonated beverage dispenser.

   D. serving fruit punch in a galvanized tub.

4. What is the *best* method for preventing a foodborne illness from seafood toxins?

   A. Purchasing smoked or cured seafood

   B. Freezing seafood prior to cooking it

   C. Purchasing seafood from approved, reputable suppliers

   D. Cooking seafood to the required minimum internal temperature

Continued on the next page...

Apply Your Knowledge	Multiple-Choice Study Questions *continued*

5. A man who ate raw oysters later became disoriented and suffered memory loss. What illness was most likely the cause?

   A. Amnesic shellfish poisoning

   B. Paralytic shellfish poisoning

   C. Neurotoxic shellfish poisoning

   D. *Vibrio vulnificus* gastroenteritis

6. Which practice will *not* prevent food from becoming contaminated?

   A. Labeling chemical spray bottles

   B. Closely inspecting food during receiving

   C. Storing products in food-grade containers

   D. Storing high-acid food away from other food

7. Which symptom will *not* occur as part of an allergic reaction to peanuts?

   A. Diarrhea

   B. Shortness of breath

   C. Swelling of the feet

   D. Reversal of hot and cold sensations

8. Which statement about mushrooms is true?

   A. Freezing will destroy toxins found in toxic wild mushrooms.

   B. Cooking will not destroy toxins found in toxic wild mushrooms.

   C. Most cases of foodborne illness occur when edible species are temperature abused.

   D. Foodborne illnesses almost always occur when mushrooms are purchased from approved suppliers.

For answers, please turn to page 3-25.

You should be aware of the following laws concerning employees who are HIV-positive (Human Immunodeficiency Virus) or have tuberculosis or hepatitis B or C:

- The Americans with Disabilities Act (ADA) provides civil-rights protection to individuals who are HIV-positive or have hepatitis B, and thus prohibits employers from firing people or transferring them out of foodhandling duties simply because they have these diseases.

- Employers must maintain the confidentiality of employees who have any nonfoodborne illness.

COMPONENTS OF A GOOD PERSONAL HYGIENE PROGRAM

Good personal hygiene is key to the prevention of foodborne illness and includes:

A Maintaining personal cleanliness

- Proper bathing
- Hair washing

B Wearing proper work attire

- Clean hat or hair restraint
- Clean clothing
- Appropriate shoes
- Removing jewelry from hands and arms

C Following hygienic hand practices

- Handwashing
- Hand maintenance
- Proper glove use

Employees must also avoid unsanitary habits and actions, maintain good health, and report wounds and illnesses.

Hygienic Hand Practices

Handwashing

Handwashing is the most critical aspect of personal hygiene. While it may appear fundamental, many foodhandlers fail to wash their hands properly and as often as needed. As a manager, it is your responsibility to train your foodhandlers and then monitor them. Never take this simple action for granted. To ensure proper handwashing in your establishment, train your foodhandlers to follow the steps illustrated in *Exhibit 4a.*

Some establishments require foodhandlers to use liquid or gel antiseptics on their hands to reduce the microorganisms on their skin. These substances must comply with Food and Drug Administration (FDA) standards and should only be used after proper handwashing—never in place of it. Once an antiseptic is applied, foodhandlers should not touch food or equipment until the substance has dried.

Foodhandlers must wash their hands before they start work and after:

- Using the restroom
- Handling raw meat, poultry and fish (before *and* after)
- Touching the hair, face, or body
- Sneezing, coughing, or using a tissue
- Smoking, eating, drinking, or chewing gum or tobacco
- Handling chemicals that might affect the safety of food
- Taking out garbage
- Clearing tables or bussing dirty dishes
- Touching clothing or aprons
- Touching anything else that may contaminate hands, such as unsanitized equipment, work surfaces, or washcloths

- **Buy gloves for different tasks.** Long gloves, for example, should be used for hand-mixing salads. Colored gloves can also be used to help prevent cross-contamination.

- **Provide a variety of glove sizes.** Gloves that are too big will not stay on the hand, and those that are too small will tear or rip easily.

- **Consider latex alternatives for employees who are sensitive to the material.**

- **Focus on safety, durability, and cleanliness.** Make sure you purchase gloves specifically designed for food contact, which include gloves bearing the NSF International certification mark. (This mark is discussed later in Section 11.)

Gloves must never be used in place of handwashing. Hands must be washed before putting gloves on and when changing to a new pair. Gloves should be removed by grasping them at the cuff and peeling them off inside out over the fingers while avoiding contact with the palm and fingers.

Foodhandlers should change their gloves:

- As soon as they become soiled or torn

- Before beginning a different task

- At least every four hours during continual use, and more often when necessary

- After handling raw meat and before handling cooked or ready-to-eat food

Check your local requirements.

How This Relates to Me...
What are the requirements for glove use in your jurisdiction?

Maintaining Personal Cleanliness

In addition to following proper hand maintenance practices, foodhandlers must maintain personal cleanliness. They should take a bath or shower before work. Foodhandlers must also keep their hair clean, since oily, dirty hair can harbor pathogens.

Proper Work Attire

A foodhandler's attire plays an important role in the prevention of foodborne illness. Dirty clothes may harbor pathogens and give customers a bad impression of your establishment. Therefore, managers should make sure that foodhandlers observe strict dress standards.

Foodhandlers should:

A **Wear a clean hat or other hair restraint.** A hair restraint will keep hair away from food and keep the foodhandler from touching it. Foodhandlers with facial hair should also wear a beard restraint.

B **Wear clean clothing daily.** If possible, foodhandlers should change into their work clothes at the establishment.

C **Remove aprons when leaving food-preparation areas.** For example, aprons should be removed and properly stored prior to taking out garbage or using the restroom.

D **Remove jewelry from hands and arms prior to preparing or serving food and when working around food-preparation areas.** Jewelry may contain microorganisms and can tempt foodhandlers to touch it. Wearing jewelry may also pose a hazard when working around equipment. Remove rings (except for a plain band); bracelets (including medical information jewelry); and watches. Your company may also require you to remove other types of jewelry, including earrings, necklaces, and facial jewelry (such as nose rings).

E **Wear appropriate shoes.** Foodhandlers should wear clean, closed-toe shoes with a sensible, nonskid sole.

Check with your local regulatory agency regarding requirements. These requirements should be reflected in written policies that are consistently monitored and enforced. All potential employees should be made aware of these policies prior to employment.

How This Relates to Me...

What are the requirements for a foodhandler's work attire in your jurisdiction?

_____

_____

_____

Policies Regarding Eating, Drinking, Chewing Gum, and Tobacco

Small droplets of saliva can contain thousands of disease-causing microorganisms. In the process of eating, drinking, chewing gum, or smoking, saliva can be transferred to the foodhandler's hands or directly to food being handled.

Foodhandlers must not:

- Smoke
- Chew gum or tobacco
- Eat or drink

When:

- Preparing or serving food
- Working in food-preparation areas
- Working in areas used to clean utensils and equipment

Some jurisdictions allow employees to drink from a covered container with a straw while in these areas. **Check with your local regulatory agency.** Foodhandlers should eat, drink, chew gum, or use tobacco products only in designated areas, such as an employee break room. They should never be allowed to spit in the establishment.

If food must be tasted during preparation, it must be placed in a separate dish and tasted with a clean utensil. The dish and utensil should then be removed from the food-preparation area for cleaning and sanitizing.

How This Relates to Me...

Does your jurisdiction allow employees to drink in food-preparation and dishwashing areas?

____ Yes   ____ No

If so, what are the requirements?

_____

_____

_____

Exhibit 4c

Employee Illnesses

Encourage foodhandlers to report health problems before working.

Policies for Reporting Illness and Injury

Foodhandlers must be encouraged to report health problems to the manager of the establishment before working. (See *Exhibit 4c.*) If they become ill while working, they must immediately report their condition. Additionally, if food or equipment could become contaminated, the foodhandler must stop working and see a doctor. There are several instances when a foodhandler must either be restricted from working with or around food or excluded from working within the establishment. (See *Exhibit 4d.*) **Check your local requirements.**

If a foodhandler must refrigerate medication while working, and it will be stored with food, he or she must place it inside a covered, leak-proof container that is clearly labeled.

Any cuts, burns, boils, sores, skin infections, or infected wounds should be reported to the manager. They should be covered with a bandage when the foodhandler is working with or around food or food-contact surfaces. Bandages should be clean and dry and must prevent leakage from the wound. As previously mentioned, disposable gloves or finger cots should be worn over bandages on hands. Foodhandlers wearing bandages may need to be temporarily reassigned to duties not involving contact with food or food-contact surfaces.

Exhibit 4d

Handling Employee Illnesses	
If	**Then**
The foodhandler has a sore throat with fever.	**Restrict the employee from working with or around food.** **Exclude the employee from the establishment if you primarily serve a high-risk population.**
The foodhandler has one or more of the following symptoms: ■ Vomiting ■ Diarrhea ■ Jaundice	**Exclude the employee from the establishment.** If the person is vomiting or has diarrhea, do not allow the individual to return to work unless he or she: ■ Has been symptom-free for twenty-four hours, **or** ■ Has a written release from a medical practitioner Do not allow employees with jaundice to return to work unless they have a written release from a medical practitioner.
The foodhandler has been diagnosed with a foodborne illness caused by one of the following pathogens: ■ *Salmonella* Typhi ■ *Shigella* spp. ■ Shiga toxin-producing *E. coli* ■ Hepatitis A virus ■ Norovirus	**Exclude the employee from the establishment and notify the local regulatory agency.** Work with the employee's medical practitioner and/or the local regulatory agency to determine when the person can safely return to work.

How This Relates to Me...

In your jurisdiction, when must employees be restricted from working with or around food?

_____

_____

In your jurisdiction, when should employees be excluded from the establishment?

_____

_____

Apply Your Knowledge

Write an **E** next to the statement if the foodhandler must be excluded from the establishment or an **R** if the person should be restricted from working with or around food.

Exclusion or Restriction?

____ **1** Bill, a line cook at a family restaurant, has a sore throat with a fever.

____ **2** Joe, a prep cook, has diarrhea.

____ **3** Mary, a sous chef, has been diagnosed with hepatitis A.

For answers, please turn to page 4-25.

Exhibit 4e

Modeling Proper Personal Hygiene

Managers must model proper behavior for foodhandlers at all times.

MANAGEMENT'S ROLE IN A PERSONAL HYGIENE PROGRAM

Management plays a critical role in the effectiveness of a personal hygiene program. As a manager, your responsibilities include:

■ Establishing proper personal hygiene policies

■ Training foodhandlers on personal hygiene policies and retraining them when necessary

■ Modeling proper behavior for foodhandlers at all times (see *Exhibit 4e*)

■ Supervising food safety practices continuously and retraining foodhandlers as necessary

■ Revising policies when laws and regulations change and when changes are recognized in the science of food safety

Apply Your Knowledge

There are at least thirteen unsafe foodhandling practices in this picture. Identify them in the space provided.

What's Wrong with This Picture?

1 _____
2 _____
3 _____
4 _____
5 _____
6 _____
7 _____
8 _____
9 _____
10 _____
11 _____
12 _____
13 _____

For answers, please turn to page 4-25.

Something to Think About...   Who's Game?

A restaurant chain on the East Coast was looking for ways to increase its employees' knowledge of general food safety principles and the importance of handwashing. Management decided that, in addition to traditional training, they would hold a voluntary competition. Spurred by a chance to win a cash prize, employees formed teams and competed against each other in a test of handwashing basics and food safety knowledge. The program was a success, with most employees scoring better than 90 percent on the food safety quiz. The competition is now an annual event.

SUMMARY

Foodhandlers can contaminate food at every step in its flow through the establishment. Good personal hygiene is a critical protective measure against contamination and foodborne illness. A successful personal hygiene program depends on trained foodhandlers who possess the knowledge, skills, and attitude necessary to keep food safe.

Foodhandlers have the potential to contaminate food when they have been diagnosed with a foodborne illness, show symptoms of a gastrointestinal illness, have infected lesions, or touch anything that might contaminate their hands. They must pay close attention to what they do with their hands since simple acts such as nose picking or running fingers through the hair can contaminate food. Proper handwashing must always be practiced. This is especially important before starting work, after using the restroom, after sneezing, coughing, smoking, eating, or drinking, and before and after handling raw food. It is up to the manager to monitor handwashing to make sure it is thorough and frequent. In addition, hands need other care to ensure they will not transfer contaminants to food. Fingernails should be kept short and clean. Cuts and wounds should be covered with clean bandages. Hand cuts should also be covered with gloves or finger cots.

Gloves can create a barrier between hands and food; however, they should never be used in place of handwashing. Hands must be washed before putting on gloves and when changing to a fresh pair. Gloves worn to handle food are for a single use and should never be washed and reused. They must be changed when they become soiled or torn, when beginning a new task, and whenever contamination occurs.

All employees must maintain personal cleanliness. They should take a bath or shower before work and keep their hair clean. Prior to handling food, employees must put on clean clothing, appropriate shoes, and a clean hair restraint. They must also remove jewelry from hands and arms. Aprons should always be removed and properly stored when the employee leaves food-preparation areas.

Establishments should implement strict policies regarding eating, drinking, smoking, and chewing gum and tobacco. These activities should not be allowed when the foodhandler is preparing or serving food or working in food-preparation areas.

Employees must be encouraged to report health problems to management before working with food. If their condition could contaminate food or equipment, they must stop working and see a doctor. Managers must not allow foodhandlers to work if they have been diagnosed with a foodborne illness caused by *Salmonella* Typhi, *Shigella* spp., shiga toxin-producing *E. coli,* the hepatitis A virus, or Norovirus. Foodhandlers must also be excluded from the establishment if they have symptoms that include diarrhea, vomiting, or jaundice. Managers must restrict them from working with or around food if they have a sore throat with fever.

Management plays a critical role in the effectiveness of a personal hygiene program. By establishing a program that includes specific policies, and by training and enforcing those policies, managers can minimize the risk of employees causing a foodborne illness. Most important, managers must set a good example by modeling proper personal hygiene practices.

Apply Your Knowledge

Randall and his manager made several errors. How many can you identify?

- If you can identify only eight to twelve errors, you may need to reread this section.

- If you can identify thirteen to seventeen errors, you have a good understanding of this section.

- If you can identify seventeen or more errors, you are on your way to becoming a food safety expert.

Randall's Day

Randall is a foodhandler at a deli. It is 7:47 a.m., and he has just woken up. He is scheduled to be at work and ready to go by 8:00 a.m. When he gets out of bed, his stomach feels queasy, but he blames that on the beer he had the night before. Fortunately, Randall lives only five minutes from work, but he does not have enough time to take a shower. He grabs the same uniform he wore the day before when prepping chicken. He also puts on his watch and several rings.

Randall does not have luck on his side today. On the way to the restaurant, his oil light comes on and he is forced to pull off the road and add oil to his car. When he walks through the door at work, he realizes he has left his hat at home. Randall is greeted by an angry manager who puts him to work right away, loading the rotisserie with raw chicken. He then moves to serving a customer who orders a freshly made salad. Randall is known for his salads and makes the salad to the customer's approval.

The deli manager, short staffed on this day, asks Randall to take out the garbage and then prepare potato salad for the lunch-hour rush. On the way back from the garbage run, Randall mentions to the manager that his stomach is bothering him. The manager, thinking of his staff shortage, asks Randall to stick it out as long as he can. Randall agrees and heads to the restroom in hope of relieving his symptoms. After quickly rinsing his hands in the restroom, he finds that the paper towels have run out. Short of time, he wipes his hands on his apron.

Later, Randall cuts his finger while preparing the potato salad. He bandages the cut and continues his prep work. The manager then summons Randall to clean the few tables in the deli that are available for customers. He puts on a pair of single-use gloves and cleans and sanitizes the tables. When finished, Randall grabs a piece of chicken from the rotisserie for a snack and immediately goes back to preparing the potato salad since it is almost noon.

For answers, please turn to page 4-26.

Apply Your Knowledge   **Notes**

Take It Back*

The following food safety concepts from this section should be taught to your employees:

- Proper handwashing
- Proper hand care
- Proper glove use

- Proper work attire
- Employee illness
- Personal practices that can lead to contamination

The tools below can be used to teach these concepts in fifteen minutes or less using the directions below. Each tool includes content and language appropriate for employees. Choose the tool or tools that work best.

Tool #1:	Tool #2:	Tool #3:	Tool #4:
ServSafe Video 3: *Personal Hygiene*	*ServSafe Employee Guide*	ServSafe Posters and Quiz Sheets	ServSafe Fact Sheets and Optional Activities

Proper Handwashing

Video segment on proper handwashing

1 Show employees the segment.

2 Ask employees to identify when hands must be washed and describe the proper procedure for handwashing.

Section 2

When and How to Wash Your Hands

1 Discuss with employees when hands must be washed and the proper procedure for handwashing.

2 Complete the Washing Order activity.

Poster: When and How to Wash Your Hands

1 Discuss with employees when hands must be washed and the proper procedure for handwashing as presented in the poster.

2 Have employees complete the Quiz Sheet: When and How to Wash Your Hands.

Proper Handwashing Fact Sheet

1 Pass out a Fact Sheet to each employee. Explain when hands must be washed and the proper procedure for handwashing using the Fact Sheet.

2 Have employees complete one or two of the Optional Activities.

* Visit the Food Safety Resource Center at *www.ServSafe.com/FoodSafety/resource* to download free posters, quiz sheets, fact sheets, and optional activities and to learn how to obtain *Employee Guides* and videos/DVDs.

Take It Back*

Tool #1: ServSafe Video 3: *Personal Hygiene*	Tool #2: *ServSafe Employee Guide*	Tool #3: ServSafe Posters and Quiz Sheets	Tool #4: ServSafe Fact Sheets and Optional Activities
Proper Hand Care			
Video segment on proper hand care 1 Show employees the segment. 2 Ask employees to identify proper hand care practices that should be followed before coming to work.	**Section 2** **Good Personal Hygiene** Discuss with employees proper hand care practices.	**Poster: Before You Come to Work…** 1 Discuss with employees hand care practices as presented in the poster. 2 Have employees complete the Quiz Sheet: Before You Come To Work…	**Hand Care Fact Sheet** 1 Pass out a Fact Sheet to each employee. Explain hand care requirements using the Fact Sheet. 2 Have employees complete the Optional Activity.
Proper Glove Use			
Video segment on using gloves properly 1 Show employees the segment. 2 Ask employees to identify when gloves should be changed.	**Section 2** **How to Use Gloves Properly** Discuss with employees the requirements for proper glove use.		**Proper Glove Use Fact Sheet** 1 Pass out a Fact Sheet to each employee. Explain proper glove use requirements using the Fact Sheet. 2 Have employees complete one or two of the Optional Activities.

* Visit the Food Safety Resource Center at *www.ServSafe.com/FoodSafety/resource* to download free posters, quiz sheets, fact sheets, and optional activities and to learn how to obtain *Employee Guides* and videos/DVDs.

Take It Back* *continued*

Tool #1: ServSafe Video 3: *Personal Hygiene*	Tool #2: *ServSafe Employee Guide*	Tool #3: ServSafe Posters and Quiz Sheets	Tool #4: ServSafe Fact Sheets and Optional Activities
Proper Work Attire			
Video segment on personal cleanliness and attire 1 Show employees the segment. 2 Ask employees to identify what should and should not be worn at work.	**Section 2** **Good Personal Hygiene Practices** Discuss with employees proper work attire.	**Poster: Before You Come to Work…** 1 Discuss with employees proper work attire as presented in the poster. 2 Have employees complete the Quiz Sheet: Before You Come to Work…	**Personal Cleanliness and Proper Attire Fact Sheet** 1 Pass out a Fact Sheet to each employee. Explain work attire requirements using the Fact Sheet. 2 Have employees complete the Optional Activity.
Employee Illness			
Video segment on reporting illness and injury 1 Show employees the segment. 2 Ask employees to identify what symptons of illness must be reported to the manager.	**Section 2** **Good Personal Hygiene Practices** Discuss with employees symptoms of illness that must be reported to the manager.		**Employee Illness Fact Sheet** 1 Pass out a Fact Sheet to each employee. Explain the symptoms of illness that must be reported to the manager using the Fact Sheet. 2 Have employees complete the Optional Activity.

* Visit the Food Safety Resource Center at *www.ServSafe.com/FoodSafety/resource* to download free posters, quiz sheets, fact sheets, and optional activities and to learn how to obtain *Employee Guides* and videos/DVDs.

Take It Back*

Tool #1: ServSafe Video 3: *Personal Hygiene*	Tool #2: *ServSafe Employee Guide*	Tool #3: ServSafe Posters and Quiz Sheets	Tool #4: ServSafe Fact Sheets and Optional Activities

Personal Practices That Can Lead to Contamination

	Section 2 **How Food Can Become Contaminated** Discuss with employees practices that can lead to contamination.	**Poster: How Food Can Become Contaminated** **1** Discuss with employees practices that can lead to contamination as presented in the poster. **2** Have employees complete the Quiz Sheet: How Food Can Become Contaminated.	

* Visit the Food Safety Resource Center at *www.ServSafe.com/FoodSafety/resource* to download free posters, quiz sheets, fact sheets, and optional activities and to learn how to obtain *Employee Guides* and videos/DVDs.

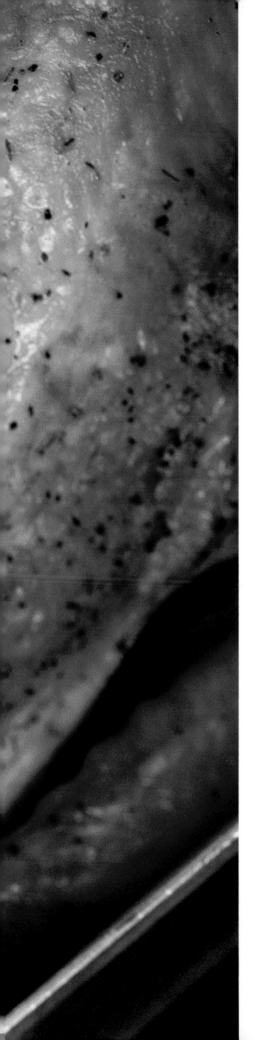

Unit 2

The Flow of Food through the Operation

5

The Flow of Food:
An Introduction

Inside this section:
- Preventing Cross-Contamination
- Time and Temperature Control
- Monitoring Time and Temperature

After completing this section, you should be able to:
- Identify methods for preventing cross-contamination.
- Identify methods for preventing time-temperature abuse.
- Identify different types of temperature-measuring devices and their uses.
- Calibrate and maintain different temperature-measuring devices.
- Properly measure the temperature of food at each point in the flow of food.

Apply Your Knowledge	Test Your Food Safety Knowledge

Check to see how much you know about the concepts in this section. Use the page references provided with each question to explore the topic.

1 **True or False:** Chicken held at an internal temperature of 125°F (52°C) has been temperature abused. *(See page 5-5.)*

2 **True or False:** Infrared thermometers are best for measuring the internal temperature of food. *(See page 5-8.)*

3 **True or False:** When checking the temperature of a roast using a bimetallic stemmed thermometer, only the tip of the thermometer stem should be inserted into the product. *(See page 5-12.)*

4 **True or False:** A thermometer calibrated by the boiling point method must be set to 135°F (57°C), after being placed in the boiling water. *(See page 5-10.)*

5 **True or False:** Washing and rinsing a cutting board will prevent it from cross-contaminating the next product placed on it. *(See page 5-4.)*

For answers, please turn to page 5-16.

CONCEPTS

- **Boiling-point method:** Method of calibrating thermometers based on the boiling point of water.

- **Calibration:** Process of ensuring that a thermometer gives accurate readings by adjusting it to a known standard, such as the freezing point or boiling point of water.

- **Flow of food:** Path food takes through an establishment, from purchasing and receiving through storing, preparing, cooking, holding, cooling, reheating, and serving.

- **Ice-point method:** Method of calibrating thermometers based on the freezing point of water.

- **Thermometer:** Device for accurately measuring the internal temperature of food, the air temperature inside a freezer or cooler, or the temperature of equipment. Bimetallic stemmed thermometers, thermocouples, and thermistors are common types of thermometers used in the restaurant and foodservice industry.

- **Time-temperature indicator (TTI):** Time and temperature monitoring device attached to a food shipment to determine if the product's temperature has exceeded safe limits during shipment or later storage.

INTRODUCTION

Your responsibility for the safety of the food in your establishment starts long before any food is actually served to the customer. Many things can happen to a product on its path through the establishment, from purchasing and receiving through storing, preparing, cooking, holding, cooling, reheating, and serving. This path is known as the flow of food. (See *Exhibit 5a.*) A frozen product that leaves the processor's plant in good condition, for example, may thaw on its way to the distributor's warehouse and go unnoticed during receiving. Once in your establishment, the product might not be stored properly or cooked to the correct internal temperature. These mistakes could cause a foodborne illness.

The safety of the food served at your establishment will depend largely on how well you apply the food safety concepts presented in this program—throughout the flow of food. To be effective, you must have a good understanding of how to prevent cross-contamination and time-temperature abuse. You must also develop a system that prioritizes, monitors, and verifies the most important food safety practices. This will be discussed in Section 10.

PREVENTING CROSS-CONTAMINATION

A major hazard in the flow of food is cross-contamination, which is the transfer of microorganisms from one food or surface to another. (See *Exhibit 5b.*) Microorganisms move around easily in a kitchen. They can be transferred from food or unwashed hands to prep tables, equipment, utensils, cutting boards, or other food.

Exhibit 5a

The Flow of Food

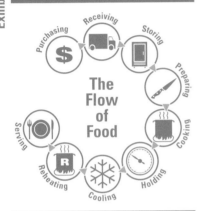

Exhibit 5b

Cross-Contamination

Cross-contamination is the transfer of microorganisms from one food or surface to another.

Cross-contamination can occur at almost any point in an operation. When you know how and where microorganisms can be transferred, cross-contamination is fairly simple to prevent. It starts with the creation of barriers between food products. These can be physical or procedural.

Physical Barriers for Preventing Cross-Contamination

■ **Assign specific equipment to each type of food product.** For example, use one set of cutting boards, utensils, and containers for poultry; another set for meat; and a third set for produce. Some manufacturers make colored cutting boards and utensils with colored handles. Color coding can tell employees which equipment to use with what products, such as green for produce, yellow for chicken, and red for meat. Although color coding minimizes the risk of cross-contamination, it does not eliminate the need to practice other methods for preventing it.

■ **Clean and sanitize all work surfaces, equipment, and utensils after each task.** After cutting up raw chicken, for example, it is not enough to simply rinse the cutting board. Wash, rinse, and sanitize cutting boards and utensils in a three-compartment sink, or run them through a warewashing machine. Make sure employees know which cleaners and sanitizers to use for each job. Sanitizers used on food-contact surfaces must meet local or state codes conforming to the Code of Federal Regulations 40CFR180.940. (See Section 11 for more information on cleaning and sanitizing.)

Procedural Barriers for Preventing Cross-Contamination

■ **When using the same prep table, prepare raw meat, fish, and poultry and ready-to-eat food at different times.** For example, establishments with limited prep space can prepare lunch salads in the morning, clean and sanitize the utensils and surfaces, and then debone chicken for dinner entrées in the same space in the afternoon.

■ **Purchase ingredients that require minimal preparation.** For example, an establishment can switch from buying raw chicken breasts to purchasing precooked frozen breasts.

The Flow of Food

Purchasing
Receiving
Storing
Preparing
Cooking
Holding
Cooling
Reheating
Serving

Take It Back*

Tool #1:	Tool #2:	Tool #3:	Tool #4:
ServSafe Video 4: *Purchasing, Receiving, and Storage*	*ServSafe Employee Guide*	ServSafe Posters and Quiz Sheets	ServSafe Fact Sheets and Optional Activities

Preventing Cross-Contamination

Video segment on preventing cross-contamination **1** Show employees the segment. **2** Ask employees to define cross-contamination and identify ways it can be prevented.	**Section 1** **How Food Can Become Unsafe** Discuss with employees cross-contamination.	**Poster: How Food Can Become Unsafe** **1** Discuss with employees cross-contamination as presented in the poster. **2** Have employees complete the Quiz Sheet: How Food Can Become Unsafe.	

* Visit the Food Safety Resource Center at *www.ServSafe.com/FoodSafety/resource* to download free posters, quiz sheets, fact sheets, and optional activities and to learn how to obtain *Employee Guides* and videos/DVDs.

Take It Back*

Tool #1: ServSafe Video 4: *Purchasing, Receiving, and Storage*	Tool #2: *ServSafe Employee Guide*	Tool #3: ServSafe Posters and Quiz Sheets	Tool #4: ServSafe Fact Sheets and Optional Activities

Calibrating a Thermometer

| | **Section 3**

How to Calibrate a Thermometer

1 Discuss with employees the procedure for calibrating a thermometer using the ice-point method.

2 Complete the Calibrate This! activity. | **Poster: How to Calibrate a Thermometer**

1 Discuss with employees the procedure for calibrating a thermometer using the ice-point method as presented in the poster.

2 Have employees complete the Quiz Sheet: How To Calibrate A Thermometer. | |

* Visit the Food Safety Resource Center at *www.ServSafe.com/FoodSafety/resource* to download free posters, quiz sheets, fact sheets, and optional activities and to learn how to obtain *Employee Guides* and videos/DVDs.

■ **Shellstock identification tags:** Each container of live, molluscan shellfish received must have an ID tag that must remain attached to the container until all the shellfish have been used. Tags must be kept on file for ninety days from the harvest date of the shellfish.

GENERAL PURCHASING AND RECEIVING PRINCIPLES

■ **Buy only from suppliers who get their products from approved sources.** An approved food source is one that has been inspected and is in compliance with applicable local, state, and federal law. Before you accept any deliveries, it is your responsibility to ensure that food you purchase comes from suppliers (distributors) and sources (points of origin) that have been approved.

■ **Make sure suppliers are reputable.** Ask other operators what their experience has been with a particular supplier.

■ **Schedule deliveries for off-peak hours and receive only one delivery at a time.** Arrange it so products are delivered when employees have adequate time to inspect them.

■ **Make sure enough trained staff are available to promptly receive, inspect, and store food.** They should be authorized to accept, reject, and sign for deliveries.

■ **Inspect deliveries carefully.** Check for proper labeling, temperature, appearance, and other factors important to safety.

■ **Use properly calibrated thermometers to sample temperatures of received food items.**

■ **Check shipments for intact packaging and signs of refreezing, prior wetness, and pest infestation.** Broken boxes, leaky packages, or dented cans are signs of mishandling and could be grounds for rejecting the shipment.

■ **Inspect deliveries immediately and put items away as quickly as possible.** This is especially true for refrigerated and frozen products.

RECEIVING AND INSPECTING FOOD

Food delivered to your establishment should be inspected carefully. Internal temperatures should be checked and recorded. (See *Exhibit 6a.*) Other conditions should be checked as well, such as color, texture, odor, and packaging. When receiving food, always follow the inspection criteria developed by your establishment.

Exhibit 6a

Checking the Temperature of Various Types of Food

Meat, Poultry, Fish

Insert the thermometer stem or probe directly into the thickest part of the product (usually the center).

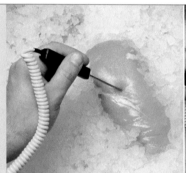

ROP and Bulk Food (MAP, Vacuum-Packed, and *Sous Vide* Food)

Insert the thermometer stem or probe between two packages.

As an alternative, it may be possible to check product temperature by folding the packaging around the thermometer stem or probe. Be careful not to puncture the packaging.

Other Packaged Food

Open the package and insert the thermometer stem or probe into the product.

The sensing area must be fully immersed in the product. The stem or probe must not touch the sides or bottom of the container.

Apply Your Knowledge

Answers

Page	Activity

6-2   Test Your Food Safety Knowledge

1. True   2. False   3. True   4. True   5. True

6-21   Accept It or Reject It

1. A	3. A	5. R	7. A	9. R
2. R	4. A	6. R	8. R	10. R

6-23   A Case in Point

1. John had good intentions and did most things correctly. However, he did make mistakes. John should have:

   A. Notified the kitchen manager that the shipment had arrived.

   B. Made sure that the bimetallic stemmed thermometer he took from the kitchen had been calibrated properly, as well as clean and sanitized, before using it.

   C. Cleaned and sanitized the thermometer after checking the temperature of each product. He should not have wiped the thermometer on his apron.

   D. Inserted the thermometer stem into the middle of the bucket of live oysters between the shellfish for an ambient reading instead of trying to judge how cold they were with his hand. The temperature of the oysters should have been 45°F (7°C) or lower.

   E. Checked the mussels and oysters with open shells by tapping on the shell to make sure they were alive.

2. A foodborne illness could have occurred because of the mistakes John made.

6-24   Multiple-Choice Study Questions

1. D	4. C	7. A	10. C
2. C	5. B	8. D	11. B
3. D	6. B	9. B	12. B

Take It Back*

The following food safety concepts from this section should be taught to your employees:

- Checking the temperature of various types of food
- When to accept or reject a delivery

The tools below can be used to teach these concepts in fifteen minutes or less using the directions below. Each tool includes content and language appropriate for employees. Choose the tool or tools that work best.

Tool #1: ServSafe Video 4: *Purchasing, Receiving, and Storage*	Tool #2: *ServSafe Employee Guide*	Tool #3: ServSafe Posters and Quiz Sheets	Tool #4: ServSafe Fact Sheets and Optional Activities

Checking the Temperature of Various Types of Food

	Section 3 **Checking the Temperature of Various Food** Discuss with employees proper thermometer placement for checking the temperature of different food items.		

* **Visit the Food Safety Resource Center at *www.ServSafe.com/FoodSafety/resource* to download free posters, quiz sheets, fact sheets, and optional activities and to learn how to obtain *Employee Guides* and videos/DVDs.**

Take It Back*

Tool #1: ServSafe Video 4: *Purchasing, Receiving, and Storage*	Tool #2: *ServSafe Employee Guide*	Tool #3: ServSafe Posters and Quiz Sheets	Tool #4: ServSafe Fact Sheets and Optional Activities

Preventing Contamination during Storage

Video segment on storage	**Section 3** **How to Properly Store Food**	**Poster: How to Store Food Properly**	**Preventing Cross-Contamination during Storage Fact Sheet**
1 Show employees the segment. **2** Ask employees what they can do to prevent contamination during storage.	Discuss with employees practices for preventing contamination during storage.	**1** Discuss with employees practices for preventing contamination during storage as presented in the poster. **2** Have employees complete the Quiz Sheet: How To Store Food Properly.	**1** Pass out a Fact Sheet to each employee. Discuss practices for preventing contamination during storage using the Fact Sheet. **2** Have employees complete one or two of the Optional Activities.

* Visit the Food Safety Resource Center at *www.ServSafe.com/FoodSafety/resource* to download free posters, quiz sheets, fact sheets, and optional activities and to learn how to obtain *Employee Guides* and videos/DVDs.

Take It Back* *continued*

Tool #1: ServSafe Video 4: *Purchasing, Receiving, and Storage*	Tool #2: *ServSafe Employee Guide*	Tool #3: ServSafe Posters and Quiz Sheets	Tool #4: ServSafe Fact Sheets and Optional Activities
Preventing Time-Temperature Abuse during Storage			
Video segment on storage 1 Show employees the segment. 2 Ask employees what they can do to prevent time-temperature abuse during storage.	**Section 3** **How to Properly Store Food** Discuss with employees practices for preventing time-temperature abuse during storage.	**Poster: How to Store Food Properly** 1 Discuss with employees practices for preventing time-temperature abuse during storage as presented in the poster. 2 Have employees complete the Quiz Sheet: How To Store Food Properly.	**Preventing Time-Temperature Abuse during Storage Fact Sheet** 1 Pass out a Fact Sheet to each employee. Discuss practices for preventing time-temperature abuse during storage using the Fact Sheet. 2 Have employees complete one or two of the Optional Activities.
Storing Food at the Proper Temperature			
			Storing Food at the Proper Temperature Fact Sheet 1 Pass out a Fact Sheet to each employee. Discuss proper storage temperatures for various food items using the Fact Sheet. 2 Have employees complete the Optional Activity.

* Visit the Food Safety Resource Center at *www.ServSafe.com/FoodSafety/resource* to download free posters, quiz sheets, fact sheets, and optional activities and to learn how to obtain *Employee Guides* and videos/DVDs.

Take It Back*

Tool #1: ServSafe Video 5: *Preparation, Cooking, and Serving*	Tool #2: *ServSafe Employee Guide*	Tool #3: ServSafe Posters and Quiz Sheets	Tool #4: ServSafe Fact Sheets and Optional Activities

Preparing Food Safely (Preventing time-temperature abuse and cross-contamination)

			Preparing Food Safely Fact Sheet 1. Pass out a Fact Sheet to each employee. Discuss practices for preventing contamination and temperature abuse during preparation using the Fact Sheet. 2. Have employees complete one or two of the Optional Activities.

Preparing Specific Food

Video segment on preparation 1. Show employees the segment. 2. Ask employees what they should do to keep salads, eggs and egg mixtures, and produce safe during preparation.			**Preparing Specific Types of Food Fact Sheet** 1. Pass out a Fact Sheet to each employee. Discuss the requirements for preparing specific types of food using the Fact Sheet. 2. Have employees complete one or two of the Optional Activities.

* Visit the Food Safety Resource Center at *www.ServSafe.com/FoodSafety/resource* to download free posters, quiz sheets, fact sheets, and optional activities and to learn how to obtain *Employee Guides* and videos/DVDs.

Take It Back* *continued*

Tool #1: ServSafe Video 5: *Preparation, Cooking, and Serving*	Tool #2: *ServSafe Employee Guide*	Tool #3: ServSafe Posters and Quiz Sheets	Tool #4: ServSafe Fact Sheets and Optional Activities
Minimum Internal Cooking Temperatures			
Video segment on specific cooking requirements **1** Show employees the segment. **2** Ask employees to identify minimum internal cooking temperatures for various food items.	**Section 4** **Minimum Internal Cooking Temperatures for Various Types of Food** **1** Discuss with employees minimum internal cooking temperatures for various food items. **2** Complete the Match Game activity.	**Poster: Minimum Internal Cooking Temperatures** **1** Discuss with employees minimum internal cooking temperatures for various food items as presented in the poster. **2** Have employees complete the Quiz Sheet: Minimum Internal Cooking Temperatures.	**Minimum Internal Cooking Temperatures Fact Sheet** **1** Pass out a Fact Sheet to each employee. Discuss minimum internal cooking temperatures for various food items using the Fact Sheet. **2** Have employees complete one or two of the Optional Activities.
Cooling and Reheating Food Safely			
Video segments on cooling food and reheating food **1** Show employees the segments. **2** Ask employees to list acceptable methods for cooling food. Ask employees to identify the requirement for reheating food properly.	**Section 4** **Proper Ways to Cool Food** **The Proper Way to Reheat Food** **1** Discuss with employees proper methods for cooling food with employees. **2** Discuss with employees the proper way to reheat food.	**Poster: Proper Ways to Cool Food** **1** Discuss the proper methods for cooling and reheating food as presented in the poster. **2** Have employees complete the Quiz Sheet: Proper Ways To Cool And Reheat Food.	**Cooling and Reheating Food Fact Sheet** **1** Pass out a Fact Sheet to each employee. Discuss the requirements for cooling and reheating food using the Fact Sheet. **2** Have employees complete one or two of the Optional Activities.

* Visit the Food Safety Resource Center at *www.ServSafe.com/FoodSafety/resource* to download free posters, quiz sheets, fact sheets, and optional activities and to learn how to obtain *Employee Guides* and videos/DVDs.

Take It Back*

Tool #1: ServSafe Video 5: *Preparation, Cooking, and Serving*	Tool #2: *ServSafe Employee Guide*	Tool #3: ServSafe Posters and Quiz Sheets	Tool #4: ServSafe Fact Sheets and Optional Activities

Preventing Contamination When Serving Food

Video segment on serving food **1** Show employees the segment. **2** Ask employees to identify the proper ways to serve food and carry utensils to prevent contamination.	**Section 4** **Proper Ways to Serve Food** Discuss with employees the proper way to serve food and carry utensils to prevent contamination.	**Poster: Proper Ways to Serve Food** **1** Discuss with employees the proper way to serve food and carry utensils as presented in the poster. **2** Have employees complete the Quiz Sheet: Proper Ways to Serve Food.	

* Visit the Food Safety Resource Center at *www.ServSafe.com/FoodSafety/resource* to download free posters, quiz sheets, fact sheets, and optional activities and to learn how to obtain *Employee Guides* and videos/DVDs.

10

Food Safety Management Systems

Inside this section:
- Prerequisite Food Safety Programs
- Active Managerial Control
- Hazard Analysis Critical Control Point (HACCP)
- Crisis Management

After completing this section, you should be able to:
- Identify how active managerial control can impact food safety.
- Identify HACCP principles for preventing foodborne illness.
- Implement HACCP principles when applicable.
- Identify when a HACCP plan is required.

- Implement a crisis management program.
- Cooperate with regulatory agencies in the event of a foodborne-illness investigation.

Apply Your Knowledge	Test Your Food Safety Knowledge
Check to see how much you know about the concepts in this section. Use the page references provided with each question to explore the topic.	**1** **True or False:** Active managerial control focuses on controlling the most common foodborne-illness risk factors identified by the Centers for Disease Control and Prevention (CDC). *(See page 10-3.)* **2** **True or False:** Purchasing fish directly from local fishermen would be considered a risk in an active managerial control system. *(See page 10-3.)* **3** **True or False:** A critical control point (CCP) is a point in the flow of food where a hazard can be prevented, eliminated, or reduced to safe levels. *(See page 10-7.)* **4** **True or False:** If cooking is a CCP for ground beef patties in a particular establishment, then ensuring the internal temperature reaches 155°F (68°C) for fifteen seconds would be an appropriate critical limit. *(See page 10-8.)* **5** **True or False:** An establishment that cures food must have a HACCP plan. *(See page 10-12.)* **For answers, please turn to page 10-22.**

CONCEPTS

■ **Food safety management system:** Group of programs, procedures, and measures designed to prevent foodborne illness by actively controlling risks and hazards throughout the flow of food.

■ **Active managerial control:** Food safety management system designed to prevent foodborne illness by addressing the five most common risk factors identified by the Centers for Disease Control and Prevention (CDC).

■ **Hazard Analysis Critical Control Point (HACCP):** Food safety management system based on the idea that if significant biological, chemical, or physical hazards are identified at specific points within a product's flow through the operation, they can be prevented, eliminated, or reduced to safe levels.

The Flow of Food

Prerequisite Food Safety Programs

Personal hygiene program

Supplier selection and specification programs

Sanitation and pest control programs

Facility design and equipment maintenance programs

Food safety training programs

INTRODUCTION

In Sections 5 through 9, you learned how to handle food safely throughout the flow of food. This accumulated knowledge will help you take the next step in preventing foodborne illness—the development of a food safety management system.

A food safety management system is a group of programs, procedures, and measures for preventing foodborne illness by actively controlling risks and hazards throughout the flow of food. Active managerial control and Hazard Analysis Critical Control Point (HACCP) offer two systematic and proactive approaches. Before these systems can be implemented, however, some prerequisite food safety programs must first be established.

PREREQUISITE FOOD SAFETY PROGRAMS

For your food safety management system to be effective, you must first have the necessary food safety programs in place. (See *Exhibit 10a*.) The principles you have learned throughout the ServSafe program will help you develop these programs. They address the basic operational and sanitation conditions within your establishment, and can include processes, policies, and procedures.

ACTIVE MANAGERIAL CONTROL

One way to manage food safety risks in your establishment is to implement active managerial control. This approach focuses on controlling the five most common risk factors responsible for foodborne illness as identified by the Centers for Disease Control and Prevention (CDC). They include:

- Purchasing food from unsafe sources
- Failing to cook food adequately
- Holding food at improper temperatures
- Using contaminated equipment
- Practicing poor personal hygiene

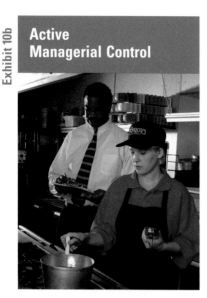

Active Managerial Control

Managers must monitor policies and procedures to ensure that they are being followed.

The Active Managerial Control Approach

There are specific steps that should be taken when using active managerial control to manage food safety risks in your establishment.

1 Consider the five risk factors as they apply throughout the flow of food and identify any issues that could impact food safety. You can use the *Food Safety Self Assessment* in the Appendix of this book to help identify issues.

2 Develop policies and procedures that address the issues that were identified. Consider input from staff when developing them. It may be necessary to provide training on these policies and procedures.

3 Regularly monitor the policies and procedures that have been developed. This proactive step—which is critical to the success of an active managerial control system—can help you determine if the policies and procedures are being followed. (See *Exhibit 10b.*) If not, it may be necessary to revise them, create new ones, or retrain employees.

4 Verify that the policies and procedures you have established are actually controlling the risk factors. Use feedback from internal sources (records, temperature logs, and self inspections) and external sources (health-inspection reports, customer comments, and quality assurance audits) to adjust the policies and procedures to continuously improve the system.

Example of Active Managerial Control

A seafood restaurant chain identified purchasing seafood from unsafe sources as a risk in their establishments. To avoid buying unsafe product, management developed a list of approved vendors based upon a predetermined set of criteria. Next, they created a policy stating that seafood could only be purchased from vendors on this list. To ensure the policy was being followed, management decided that seafood invoices and deliveries would be monitored. On a regular basis, they looked at the criteria they had established for selecting seafood vendors, to ensure that it was still appropriate for controlling the risk. They also decided to review their policy whenever a problem arose and change it if necessary.

Something to Think About...   **Get a Handle on It!**

A local health department was inspecting a store in a large quick-service chain. The inspector noticed that the grill operator who was handling raw chicken fillets also put cooked fillets in a holding drawer. A sandwich maker touched the handle of the drawer each time she retrieved a cooked fillet.

The health inspector recognized that the grill operator was contaminating the handle of the holding drawer each time he put a cooked fillet inside—since his hands had touched raw chicken. As the sandwich maker touched the contaminated handle, there was a risk that she could contaminate the sandwiches she was assembling.

While working with the unit manager to find a solution, the inspector recommended adding an extra handle to the holding drawer and designating one for each position. The chain adopted the recommendation in all of its units. After being informed of the risk posed by the contaminated equipment, the quick-service chain followed the procedure outlined by its active managerial control system. This included modifying their standard operating procedures (SOPs) to control the risk, retraining employees, and incorporating the new SOPs in the chain's monitoring program.

HAZARD ANALYSIS CRITICAL CONTROL POINT (HACCP)

A HACCP system can also be used to control risks and hazards throughout the flow of food. HACCP (pronounced *Hass-ip*) is based on the idea that if significant biological, chemical, or physical hazards are identified at specific points within a product's flow through an operation, they can be prevented, eliminated, or reduced to safe levels.

To be effective, a HACCP system must be based on a written plan that is specific to each facility's menu, customers, equipment, processes, and operations. Since each HACCP plan is unique, a plan that works for one establishment may not work for another.

The Seven HACCP Principles

1. Conduct a hazard analysis.

2. Determine critical control points (CCPs).

3. Establish critical limits.

4. Establish monitoring procedures.

5. Identify corrective actions.

6. Verify that the system works.

7. Establish procedures for record keeping and documentation.

The HACCP Approach

In order to focus on the critical aspects of the HACCP plan, it is essential that you have the necessary prerequisite food safety programs in place. These programs are the foundation upon which an effective HACCP system is built.

A HACCP plan is based on the seven basic principles outlined by the National Advisory Committee on Microbiological Criteria for Foods. (See *Exhibit 10c.*) These principles are seven sequential steps that outline how to create a HACCP plan. Since each principle builds on the information gained from the previous principle, you must consider all seven principles in order when developing your plan.

In general terms:

■ Principles One and Two help you identify and evaluate your hazards.

■ Principles Three, Four, and Five help you establish ways for controlling those hazards.

■ Principles Six and Seven help you maintain the HACCP plan and system and verify its effectiveness.

The Seven HACCP Principles

The information covered in the next several pages is designed to provide you with an introduction to the seven HACCP principles and an overview of the process for developing a HACCP program. A real-world example—highlighted in blue—has also been included for each principle. It documents the efforts of *Enrico's,* an Italian restaurant, as it implements a HACCP program.

Introduction to the Seven HACCP Principles

Principle One: Conduct a Hazard Analysis.

To identify and assess potential hazards in the food you serve, start by taking a look at how it is processed in your establishment. Many types of food are processed similarly. The most common processes include:

- Preparing and serving without cooking (salads, cold sandwiches, etc.)
- Preparing and cooking for same-day service (grilled chicken sandwiches, hamburgers, etc.)
- Preparing, cooking, holding, cooling, reheating, and serving (chili, soup, pasta sauce with meat, etc.)

Take a look at your menu and identify items that are processed similarly. Next, identify those that are potentially hazardous and determine where food safety hazards are likely to occur for each one. Hazards include contamination by:

- Bacteria, viruses, or parasites
- Cleaning compounds, sanitizers, and allergens
- General physical contaminants

The management team at *Enrico's* decided to implement a HACCP program. They began by conducting a hazard analysis.

Looking at their menu, they noted that several of their dishes—including the spicy charbroiled chicken breast—are received, stored, prepared, cooked, and served the same day.

The team determined that bacteria were the most likely hazard to food prepared by this process.

Principle Two: Determine Critical Control Points (CCPs)

Find the points in the process where the identified hazard(s) can be prevented, eliminated, or reduced to safe levels. These are the critical control points (CCPs). Depending on the process, there may be more than one CCP.

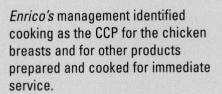

Enrico's management identified cooking as the CCP for the chicken breasts and for other products prepared and cooked for immediate service.

While these food items must be handled safely throughout the flow of food, proper cooking is the only step that will eliminate or reduce bacteria to safe levels.

Since the chicken breasts were prepared for immediate service, cooking was the only CCP identified.

Introduction to the Seven HACCP Principles

Principle Three:
Establish Critical Limits

For each CCP, establish minimum or maximum limits that must be met to prevent or eliminate the hazard, or to reduce it to a safe level.

Since cooking was identified as the CCP for *Enrico's* chicken breasts, management determined that the critical limit would be cooking the chicken to a minimum internal temperature of 165°F (74°C) for fifteen seconds.

They decided that the critical limit could be met by placing the chicken breasts in the broiler and cooking them for sixteen minutes.

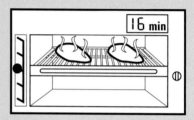

Principle Four:
Establish Monitoring Procedures

Once critical limits have been established, determine the best way for your operation to check them to make sure they are consistently met. Identify who will monitor them and how often.

Since each charbroiled chicken breast is cooked to order, *Enrico's* chose to check the critical limit by inserting a clean and sanitized thermocouple probe into the thickest part of each breast.

The grill cook is required to check the temperature of each chicken breast after cooking to ensure that it has reached the minimum internal temperature of 165°F (74°C).

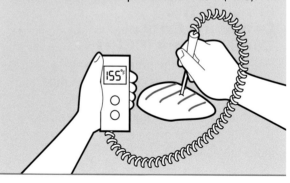

Introduction to the Seven HACCP Principles

Principle Five:
Identify Corrective Actions

Identify steps that must be taken when a critical limit is *not* met. These steps should be determined in advance.

If the chicken breast has not reached its critical limit within the sixteen-minute cook time, the grill cook at *Enrico's* must keep cooking the breast until it has.

This and all other corrective actions are noted in the temperature log.

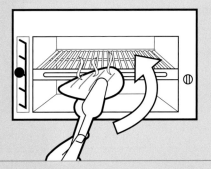

Principle Six:
Verify That the System Works

Determine if the plan is working as intended. Plan to evaluate on a regular basis your monitoring charts, records, how you performed your hazard analysis, etc., and determine if your plan adequately prevents, reduces, or eliminates identified hazards.

Enrico's management team performs HACCP checks once per shift to ensure that critical limits were met and appropriate corrective actions were taken when necessary.

Additionally, they check the temperature logs on a weekly basis to identify patterns, or to determine if processes or procedures need to be changed. For example, over several weeks they noticed that toward the end of each week, the chicken breast often failed to meet its critical limit. The appropriate corrective action was being taken; however, management discovered that *Enrico's* received chicken shipments from a different vendor on Thursdays. This vendor provided a six-ounce chicken breast instead of the four-ounce chicken breast listed in *Enrico's* chicken specifications. Management worked with the vendor to ensure they received four-ounce breasts, and changed their receiving procedure to include a weight check.

Introduction to the Seven HACCP Principles

Principle Seven:
Establish Procedures for Record Keeping and Documentation

Maintain your HACCP plan and keep all documentation created when developing it. In addition, keep records obtained when:

- Monitoring activities are performed
- Corrective action is taken
- Equipment is validated (checked to ensure it is in good working condition)
- Working with suppliers (i.e., shelf-life studies, invoices, specifications, challenge studies, etc.)

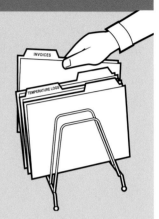

Enrico's management team determined that time-temperature logs should be kept for three months and receiving invoices for sixty days.

The team uses this documentation to support and revise their HACCP plan when necessary.

Another HACCP Example

The *Enrico's* example offers insight into the development of one type of HACCP plan. A plan may look much different when it addresses products that are processed more simply, such as those prepared and served without cooking. A good example is the HACCP plan developed by *Fresh Fruit Express,* an innovative fruit-only concept known for their signature item— the Melon Medley salad.

The HACCP team at *Fresh Fruit Express* conducted a hazard analysis for the Melon Medley Salad, which contains fresh watermelon, honeydew, and cantaloupe (Principle 1). They determined that bacteria pose a risk to the fresh-cut melons.

Since the melons are prepared, held, and served without cooking, the HACCP team determined that preparation and holding are CCPs for the salad (Principle 2). They decided that thoroughly cleaning and drying the melon's surface during preparation would reduce bacteria, and holding the melon at the proper temperature could prevent its growth. They determined that receiving is *not* a CCP since *Fresh Fruit Express* requires all melons be purchased from an approved source.

Apply Your Knowledge

Notes

damage these types of material. They also tend to be slippery when wet. Vinyl tile in particular requires a high level of maintenance, including waxing and frequent machine buffing. For this reason, it is a poor choice for dining rooms or public areas. However, vinyl tile is practical for employee dressing rooms, break rooms, and foodservice offices.

Hard-Surface Flooring

Hard-surface flooring is commonly used in establishments since it is nonabsorbent and very durable. It includes quarry and ceramic tile, brick, terrazzo, marble, and hardwood. These types of flooring are an excellent choice for public restrooms or high-soil areas—especially quarry and ceramic tile. However, there are several disadvantages to using hard-surface flooring materials because they:

- Are not resilient and may crack or chip if heavy objects are dropped on them

- Do not absorb sound

- Are somewhat difficult to clean

- May break objects dropped on them

- Can be slippery, especially if marble or a glazed tile is used (unglazed tiles, however, are more slip resistant)

- Are more expensive to install and maintain

Carpeting

Carpeting is a popular choice for some areas of the establishment, such as dining rooms, because it absorbs sound. However, it is not recommended in high-soil areas, including:

- Beverage stations

- Major traffic aisles

- Waitstaff service areas

- Tray and dish drop-off areas

Carpet can be maintained by vacuuming. Areas prone to heavy traffic and moisture will require routine cleaning. Special carpet can be purchased for areas where sanitation, moisture, and fire safety are a concern.

Exhibit 11d

Coving

Coving is placed between the floor and wall to eliminate corners or gaps that would be impossible to clean.

Special Flooring Needs

Nonslip surfaces should be used in high-traffic areas. In fact, nonslip surfaces are best for the entire kitchen, since slips and falls are a potential hazard. Rubber mats are allowed for safety reasons in areas where standing water may occur, such as the dish room. Rubber mats should be picked up and cleaned separately when scrubbing floors.

Coving is required in establishments using resilient or hard-surface flooring materials. Coving is a curved, sealed edge placed between the floor and the wall to eliminate sharp corners or gaps that would be impossible to clean. (See *Exhibit 11d*.) The coving tile or strip must adhere tightly to the wall to eliminate hiding places for insects. This will also prevent moisture from deteriorating the wall.

CONSIDERATIONS FOR SPECIFIC AREAS OF THE FACILITY

Handwashing Stations

Handwashing stations must be conveniently located so employees will be encouraged to wash their hands often. They are required in restrooms, and areas used for food preparation, service, and dishwashing. These stations must be operable, stocked, and maintained. A handwashing station must be equipped with the following items (see *Exhibit 11e*):

- **Hot and cold running water.** Hot and cold water should be supplied through a mixing valve or combination faucet at a temperature of at least 100°F (38°C).

- **Soap.** The soap can be liquid, bar, or powder. Liquid soap is generally preferred, and some local codes require it.

- **A means to dry hands.** Most local codes require establishments to supply disposable paper towels in handwashing stations. Installing at least one warm-air dryer will provide an alternate method for drying hands if paper towels run out. Continuous-cloth towel systems, if allowed, should be used only if the unit is working properly and the towel rolls are checked and changed regularly. The use of common cloth towels is not permitted because they can transmit contaminants from one person's hands to another.

Sanitary Facilities   Cleaning & Sanitizing   Integrated Pest Mgmt.

- **Waste container.** Waste containers are required if disposable paper towels are provided.

- **Signage indicating employees are required to wash hands before returning to work.** The sign should reflect all languages used in the establishment.

How This Relates to Me...

What are the requirements for a handwashing station in your jurisdiction?

_____

_____

Exhibit 11e

Acceptable Handwashing Station

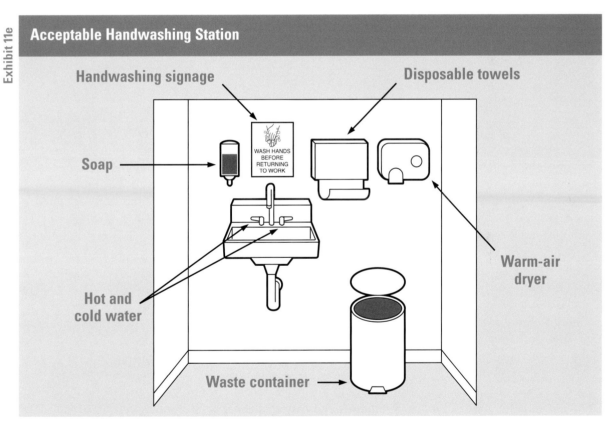

A handwashing station must be equipped with hot and cold running water, soap, a means to dry hands, a waste container (if disposable towels are used), and signage reminding employees to wash hands.

Apply Your Knowledge	What's Missing?

This handwashing station is missing four items. Can you identify what's missing?

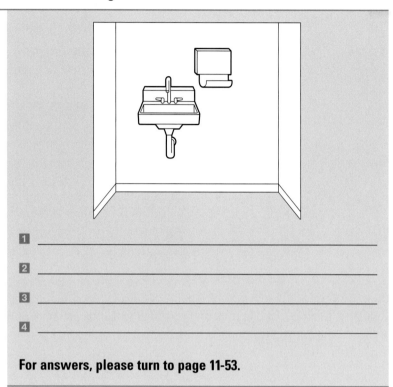

1 _____

2 _____

3 _____

4 _____

For answers, please turn to page 11-53.

SANITATION STANDARDS FOR EQUIPMENT

It is important to purchase equipment that has been designed with sanitation in mind. Food-contact surfaces must be:

- Safe

- Durable

- Corrosion resistant

- Nonabsorbent

- Sufficient in weight and thickness to withstand repeated cleaning

- Smooth and easy to clean

- Resistant to pitting, chipping, crazing (spider cracks), scratching, scoring, distortion, and decomposition

■ Rinsing, swabbing, or spraying them with a specific concentration of sanitizing solution

In some instances, detergent-sanitizer blends may be used to sanitize surfaces, but they still must be cleaned and rinsed first. Scented or oxygen bleaches are not acceptable as sanitizers for food-contact surfaces. Household bleaches are acceptable only if the labels indicate they have been registered by the EPA.

Factors Influencing the Effectiveness of Sanitizers

Several factors influence the effectiveness of chemical sanitizers. The most critical include:

■ **Concentration.** Chemical sanitizers are mixed with water until the proper concentration—ratio of sanitizer to water—is reached. Mixing the sanitizer to the proper concentration is critical, since concentrations below those required in your jurisdiction or recommended by the manufacturer could fail to sanitize objects. Concentrations higher than recommended can be unsafe, leave an odor or bad taste on objects, and may corrode metals. Concentration is measured using a sanitizer test kit and is expressed in parts per million (ppm). (See *Exhibit 11n.*) The test kit should be designed for the sanitizer you are using and is usually available from the manufacturer or your supplier. The concentration of a sanitizing solution must be checked frequently since the sanitizer is depleted during use. Hard water, food particles, and detergent inadequately rinsed from a surface can quickly reduce the sanitizer's effectiveness. A sanitizing solution must be changed when it is visibly dirty, or when its concentration has dropped below the required level.

■ **Temperature.** Follow manufacturers' recommendations for the proper temperature.

■ **Contact time.** For a sanitizing solution to kill microorganisms, it must make contact with the object for a specific amount of time.

See *Exhibit 11o* on the next page for general guidelines for the effective use of chlorine, iodine, and quats.

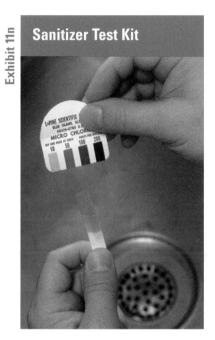

Exhibit 11n

Sanitizer Test Kit

Use a test kit to check the concentration of a sanitizing solution.

Section 11   Sanitary Facilities and Pest Management

Exhibit 11o

General Guidelines for the Effective Use of Chlorine, Iodine, and Quats					
Chlorine				**Iodine**	**Quats**
Temperature					
120°F (49°C)	100°F (38°C)	75°F (24°C)	55°F (13°C)	75°F (24°C)	75°F (24°C)
Concentration					
25 ppm	50 ppm	50 ppm	100 ppm	12.5 to 25 ppm	As per manufacturers' recommendations
pH					
<8–10	<10	<8	<8–10	≤5	As per manufacturers' recommendations
Contact Time					
10 sec	7 sec	7 sec	10 sec	30 sec	30 sec

MACHINE DISHWASHING

Most tableware, utensils, and even pots and pans can be cleaned and sanitized in a dishwashing machine. Dish machines sanitize by using either hot water or a chemical sanitizing solution.

High-Temperature Machines

High-temperature machines rely on hot water to clean and sanitize. Water temperature is critical. If the water is *not* hot enough, items will not be properly sanitized. If the water is too hot, it may vaporize before tableware and utensils have been sanitized. Extremely hot water can also bake food onto these items.

The temperature of the final sanitizing rinse must be at least 180°F (82°C). For stationary rack, single-temperature machines, it must be at least 165°F (74°C). The dishwasher must be equipped with a built-in thermometer that measures water temperature at the manifold—the point where the water sprays into the tank. Establishments that clean and sanitize high

volumes of tableware may need to install a heating device to keep up with the demand for hot water.

Chemical-Sanitizing Machines

Chemical-sanitizing machines can clean and sanitize items at much lower temperatures, but not lower than 120°F (49°C). Since different sanitizers require different rinse-water temperatures, it is important to follow the dishwashing temperature guidelines, provided by the manufacturer.

Dishwashing-Machine Operation

All dishwashing machines should be operated according to the recommendations provided by the manufacturer. No matter what type of machine you use, however, there are general procedures to follow when cleaning and sanitizing tableware, utensils, and related items.

- **Check the machine for cleanliness at least once a day, cleaning it as often as needed.** Fill tanks with clean water. Clear detergent trays and spray nozzles of food and foreign objects. Use an acid cleaner on the machine whenever necessary to remove mineral deposits caused by hard water. Make sure detergent and sanitizer dispensers are properly filled.

- **Scrape, rinse, or soak items before washing.** Presoak items with dried-on food.

- **Load dish racks correctly.** Make sure all surfaces are exposed to the spray action. Use racks designed for the items being washed, and never overload them. (See *Exhibit 11p*.)

- **Check temperatures and pressure.** Follow manufacturers' recommendations.

Exhibit 11p

Loading Dish Racks

Never overload dish racks, and make sure all surfaces are exposed to the spray action of the dishwasher.

■ **Check each rack as it comes out of the machine for soiled items.** Run dirty items through again until they are clean. Most items will need only one pass if the water temperature is correct and proper procedures are followed.

■ **Air-dry all items.** Towels can recontaminate items.

■ **Keep your dishwashing machine in good repair.**

CLEANING AND SANITIZING IN A THREE-COMPARTMENT SINK

Establishments that do not have a dishwashing machine may use a three-compartment sink to wash items (some local regulatory agencies allow the use of two-compartment sinks; others require four-compartment sinks). These sinks are often used to wash larger items. A properly set-up station includes:

■ An area for rinsing away food or for scraping food into garbage containers

■ Drain boards to hold both soiled and clean items

■ A thermometer to measure water temperature

■ A clock with a second hand that allows employees to time how long items have been immersed in the sanitizing sink

Before cleaning and sanitizing items in a three-compartment sink, each sink and all work surfaces must be cleaned and sanitized. Follow the steps listed below when cleaning and sanitizing tableware, utensils, and equipment. (See *Exhibit 11q.*)

1 **Rinse, scrape, or soak all items before washing.**

2 **Wash items in the first sink in a detergent solution at least 110°F (43°C).** Use a brush, cloth, or nylon scrub pad to loosen the remaining soil. Replace the detergent solution when the suds are gone or the water is dirty.

3 **Immerse or spray-rinse items in the second sink.** Remove all traces of food and detergent. If using the immersion method, replace the rinse water when it becomes cloudy or dirty.

Take It Back*

Tool #1: ServSafe Video 6: *Facilities, Cleaning and Sanitizing, and Pest Management*	Tool #2: *ServSafe Employee Guide*	Tool #3: ServSafe Posters and Quiz Sheets	Tool #4: ServSafe Fact Sheets and Optional Activities

How to Make Sure Sanitizers Are Effective

Video segment on sanitizing methods **1** Show employees the segment. **2** Ask employees to identify the three factors that determine the effectiveness of a sanitizer.	**Section 5** **How to Make Sure That Sanitizers Are Effective** Discuss with employees the three factors that determine the effectiveness of a sanitizer.		

Cleaning and Sanitizing in a Three-Compartment Sink

Video segment on dishwashing in a three-compartment sink **1** Show employees the segment. **2** Ask employees to identify the proper steps for cleaning and sanitizing items in a three-compartment sink.	**Section 5** **How to Clean and Sanitize in a Three-Compartment Sink** **1** Discuss with employees the proper steps for cleaning and sanitizing in a three-compartment sink. **2** Complete the What's Your Order? activity.	**Poster: How to Clean and Sanitize in a Three-Compartment Sink** **1** Discuss with employees the proper steps for cleaning and sanitizing in a three-compartment sink. **2** Have employees complete the Quiz Sheet: How To Clean And Sanitize In A Three-Compartment Sink.	

* Visit the Food Safety Resource Center at *www.ServSafe.com/FoodSafety/resource* to download free posters, quiz sheets, fact sheets, and optional activities and to learn how to obtain *Employee Guides* and videos/DVDs.

Take It Back*

Tool #1: ServSafe Video 6: *Facilities, Cleaning and Sanitizing, and Pest Management*	Tool #2: *ServSafe Employee Guide*	Tool #3: ServSafe Posters and Quiz Sheets	Tool #4: ServSafe Fact Sheets and Optional Activities

How to Store Cleaning Supplies

Video segment on storing cleaning tools and supplies 1 Show employees the segment. 2 Ask employees to identify the proper way to store cleaning tools and supplies.	**Section 5** **How to Store Cleaning Supplies** Discuss with employees the proper procedure for storing cleaning supplies.		

* Visit the Food Safety Resource Center at *www.ServSafe.com/FoodSafety/resource* to download free posters, quiz sheets, fact sheets, and optional activities and to learn how to obtain *Employee Guides* and videos/DVDs.

Notes

Food Safety Regulation and Standards

Inside this section:
- Government Regulatory System for Food
- The *FDA Food Code*
- The Inspection Process
- Self Inspections

After completing this section, you should be able to:
- Identify the principles and procedures needed to comply with food safety regulations.
- Identify state and local regulatory agencies and regulations that require food safety compliance.
- Prepare for a regulatory inspection.
- Identify the proper procedures for guiding a health inspector through the establishment.

Apply Your Knowledge	Test Your Food Safety Knowledge

Check to see how much you know about the concepts in this section. Use the page references provided with each question to explore the topic.

1 **True or False:** The Food and Drug Administration (FDA) issues food regulations that must be followed by each establishment. *(See page 12-4.)*

2 **True or False:** Health inspectors are employees of the Centers for Disease Control and Prevention (CDC). *(See page 12-4.)*

3 **True or False:** You should ask to accompany the health inspector during the inspection of your establishment. *(See page 12-8.)*

4 **True or False:** Critical violations noted during a health inspection usually must be corrected within one week of the inspection. *(See page 12-6.)*

5 **True or False:** Establishments can be closed by the health department if they find a significant lack of refrigeration. *(See page 12-10.)*

For answers, please turn to page 12-15.

CONCEPTS

- **U.S. Department of Agriculture (USDA):** Federal agency responsible for the inspection and quality grading of meat, meat products, poultry, dairy products, eggs and egg products, and fruit and vegetables shipped across state lines.

- **Food and Drug Administration (FDA):** Federal agency that issues the *FDA Food Code* working jointly with the USDA and the Centers for Disease Control and Prevention (CDC). The FDA also inspects foodservice operations that cross state borders—such as food manufacturers and processors, and foodservice on planes and trains—because they overlap the jurisdictions of two or more states. In addition, the FDA shares responsibility with the USDA for inspecting food-processing plants to ensure standards of purity, wholesomeness, and compliance with labeling requirements.

Apply Your Knowledge

Use these questions to test your knowledge of the concepts presented in this section.

Multiple-Choice Study Questions

1. An establishment can be closed for all of these reasons *except*
   A. significant lack of refrigeration.
   B. backup of sewage.
   C. significant infestation of insects or rodents.
   D. minor violations not corrected within forty-eight hours or less.

2. Which is a goal of the food safety inspection program?
   A. To evaluate whether an establishment is meeting minimum food safety standards
   B. To protect the public's health
   C. To convey new food safety information to establishments
   D. All of the above

3. Which operation would most likely be subject to a food safety inspection by a federal agency?
   A. Hospital
   B. Passenger train traveling from New York to Chicago
   C. Local ice cream store with a history of food safety violations
   D. Food kitchen run by church volunteers

4. A person shows up at a restaurant claiming to be a health inspector. What should the manager do?
   A. Ask to see identification.
   B. Ask to see an inspection warrant.
   C. Ask for a hearing to determine if the inspection is necessary.
   D. Ask for a one-day postponement to prepare for the inspection.

5. Which agency enforces food safety in a restaurant?
   A. FDA
   B. CDC
   C. State or local health department
   D. USDA

Continued on the next page...

Apply Your Knowledge

Multiple-Choice Study Questions *continued*

6. Violations noted on the health inspection report should be
   A. discussed in detail with the inspector.
   B. corrected within forty-eight hours or when indicated by the inspector if they are critical.
   C. explored to determine why they occurred.
   D. All of the above

7. The responsibility for keeping food safe in an establishment rests with the
   A. FDA.
   B. manager/operator.
   C. health inspector.
   D. state health department.

8. Food regulations developed by state agencies are
   A. minimum standards necessary to ensure food safety.
   B. maximum standards necessary to ensure food safety.
   C. voluntary guidelines for establishments to follow.
   D. inspection practices for grading meats and meat products.

For answers, please turn to page 12-15.

Apply Your Knowledge   Answers

Page	Activity
12-2	Test Your Food Safety Knowledge

1. False   2. False   3. True   4. False   5. True

12-13   Multiple-Choice Study Questions

1. D   3. B   5. C   7. B
2. D   4. A   6. D   8. A

13

Employee Food Safety Training

Inside this section:
- Initial and Ongoing Employee Training
- Delivering Training
- Training Follow-Up
- Food Safety Certification

After completing this section, you should be able to:
- Recognize a manager's responsibility to provide food safety training to employees.
- Identify the need to maintain food safety training records.
- Identify appropriate training tools for teaching food safety.
- Recognize that foodhandlers require initial and ongoing food safety training.

Apply Your Knowledge	Test Your Food Safety Knowledge
Check to see how much you know about the concepts in this section. Use the page references provided with each question to explore the topic.	**1** **True or False:** A major advantage of Web-based food safety training is that the content is delivered the same way every time. *(See page 13-15.)* **2** **True or False:** An employee who receives food safety training upon being hired does not require further training. *(See page 13-4.)* **3** **True or False:** Training videos will be less effective if the trainer stops them at different points to discuss the concepts presented. *(See page 13-15.)* **4** **True or False:** It is important for legal reasons to keep records of food safety training conducted at the establishment. *(See page 13-4.)* **5** **True or False:** It is the manager's responsibility to provide employees with food safety training. *(See page 13-4.)* **For answers, please turn to page 13-23.**

CONCEPTS

- **Training need:** Gap between what employees are required to know to do their jobs and what they actually know. There are several ways to identify food safety training needs including observing job performance, testing food safety knowledge, and surveying employees to identify areas of weakness.

- **Training objective:** Statement that describes what employees should be able to do after training has been completed. They serve as the guide when delivering content, and therefore, must be clearly defined and measurable.

- **Training plan:** Specific list of events that will take place during the training session. Training plans should include the specific learning objectives, a list of training tools needed during the training session, and specific talking points that should be covered.

- **Training delivery methods:** Approaches for providing training to employees. This can include more traditional methods such as lectures, demonstrations or role-play, or more technology-based approaches such as Web-based training and interactive CD-ROMs. Regardless of the approach, it is important to use more than one method of delivery since employees learn differently.

- **Evaluation:** Methods used to determine if employees have the knowledge and skills needed to meet the objectives of the training program. Written, oral, and performance-based tests are often used.

INTRODUCTION

Training in the establishment is difficult at best. Time, tools, and resources are often lacking. In addition, managers are faced with turnover and staffing problems that frequently take precedence. Training can also be costly. It often takes staff away from regular tasks. Sometimes it requires the use of Web-based programs, or the services of professional trainers. Typically, it involves the use of training tools to reinforce knowledge, such as videos, slides, books, and CD-ROMs. However, food safety training will have a positive return on investment in the long run. The benefits can include:

- **Avoiding the costs associated with a foodborne-illness outbreak.** These costs can be significant and may include legal fees and medical bills.

- **Preventing the loss of revenue and reputation resulting from a foodborne-illness outbreak.** These losses can have a devastating impact on an establishment.

- **Improving employee morale and reducing turnover.** Most employees want to do the job right and expect to receive training.

- **Increasing customer satisfaction.** When customers see an establishment is committed to serving safe food, satisfaction will be higher.

Exhibit 13a

Identifying Training Needs

Training needs can be identified by observing employee job performance.

Exhibit 13b

Food Safety Training

All employees require general food safety knowledge, while some knowledge will be specific to the job position.

INITIAL AND ONGOING EMPLOYEE TRAINING

As a manager, it is your responsibility to ensure that employees have the knowledge and skills needed to handle food safely in your establishment. You must also keep them informed of changes in the science of food safety and best practices in the industry.

Your first task is to assess the training needs in your establishment. A training need is a gap between what employees are required to know to perform their jobs and what they actually know. For new hires, the need might be apparent. For employees already on staff, the need is not always obvious.

Identifying food safety training needs may require work. There are several ways to accomplish this which can include:

- Testing employees' food safety knowledge

- Observing employees' performance on the job (see *Exhibit 13a*)

- Surveying employees to identify areas of weakness

All employees require general food safety knowledge. Other knowledge will be specific to the tasks performed on the job. For example, all employees need to know the proper way to wash their hands, but only dishwashers need to know how to load a dishrack to ensure items are properly cleaned and sanitized. (See *Exhibit 13b*.)

It is dangerous to assume new employees will understand your establishment's food safety procedures without proper training. From their first day on the job, they should understand the importance of food safety and should receive training in several critical areas. (See *Exhibit 13c*.)

Regardless of their position, employees need to be retrained periodically on these food safety practices. This can be accomplished by scheduling short retraining sessions, holding meetings to update staff on new procedures, or conducting motivational sessions that reinforce food safety practices.

Keep records of all food safety training conducted at your establishment. For legal reasons, it is important to document that employees have completed this training.

Critical Food Safety Knowledge for Employees

Proper personal hygiene

- Maintaining health
- Personal cleanliness
- Proper work attire
- Hygienic practices (including handwashing)

Safe food preparation

- Time-temperature control
- Preventing cross-contamination
- Handling food safely during:
    - Preparation and cooking
    - Holding and cooling
    - Reheating and service

Proper cleaning and sanitizing

- Procedures for cleaning and sanitizing food-contact surfaces

Safe chemical handling

- Procedures for safely handling chemicals used in the establishment

Pest identification and prevention

To be successful, a food safety training program requires these essential elements:

- **Clearly defined and measurable objectives.** Training objectives need to be identified before any training takes place. Training objectives are statements that describe what employees should be able to do after training has been completed. They should be clearly defined and measurable. For example, if you want employees to be able to wash their hands according to the five steps outlined in *ServSafe Essentials,* then a clearly defined training objective might state: **Employees will be able to wash their hands following the five steps for proper handwashing.**

- **Training that supports the objectives.** Training objectives serve as a guide for delivering content. The content should follow the objectives closely. Content that goes beyond the scope of your training objectives burdens employees with nonessential information. It also wastes time and money. Content that fails to meet objectives results in employees who are not prepared to handle food safely.

- **Evaluation to ensure the objectives have been achieved.** Evaluation is important because it tells you if training has provided employees with the knowledge and skills needed to handle food safely. To evaluate training, you must carefully compare employee performance to the training objectives. There are several ways in which employee performance can be measured. It is often measured through written or oral tests. (See *Exhibit 13d.*) It can also be measured by evaluating the employee while he or she performs a task required by the objective. In the handwashing example, the best way to measure whether employees can wash their hands properly might be to evaluate them while they wash their hands. During the evaluation, you would watch to see if they accurately followed the five steps for proper handwashing.

- **A work climate that reinforces training.** The work climate will have a dramatic impact on whether employees will do what they have been trained to do. If there are penalties for doing things the right way, employees may be less likely to follow through on the job. For example, employees may not

Exhibit 13d

Evaluation

Written tests can be used to evaluate whether employees have the knowledge to handle food safely.

change disposable gloves when necessary if they are continually disciplined for "wasting" gloves. They also will be less likely to follow the proper practices if they are not reinforced on the job. For example, a foodhandler may begin to wear bracelets and rings to work after she begins to see that coworkers are not penalized for doing so. Employees may also have a difficult time doing what they have been trained to do when the proper tools are not available. For example, if thermometers are broken or not available, an employee cannot spotcheck the temperature of food during the receiving process.

- **Management support.** When it comes to training, never underestimate the importance of leading by example. Employees must see that the establishment's commitment to food safety comes from the top down. If managers show that commitment through behavior and attitude, employees are likely to follow. (See *Exhibit 13e.*)

DELIVERING TRAINING

Before any training actually occurs, you should start with the necessary planning. This includes choosing appropriate training-delivery methods (covered later in this section), selecting training materials, and determining the best method for evaluating employee knowledge after the session has ended. Planning also includes making administrative decisions, such as where to hold the training and how to schedule it.

Once these decisions have been made, the next step is to create an agenda or training plan. A training plan is a very specific list of events that will take place during the training session. When developing a training plan, you should list:

- **Specific learning objective(s).**

- **Training tools needed for the session.** This may include books, audiovisual materials, and food safety equipment or props.

- **Specific training points that should be covered.** The training plan should also identify the amount of time that should be spent on each point.

Exhibit 13e

Leading by Example

If managers show a commitment to food safety through behavior and attitude, employees are likely to follow.

A sample training plan for calibrating a thermometer has been included in *Exhibit 13f.*

Sample Training Plan for Calibrating a Thermometer

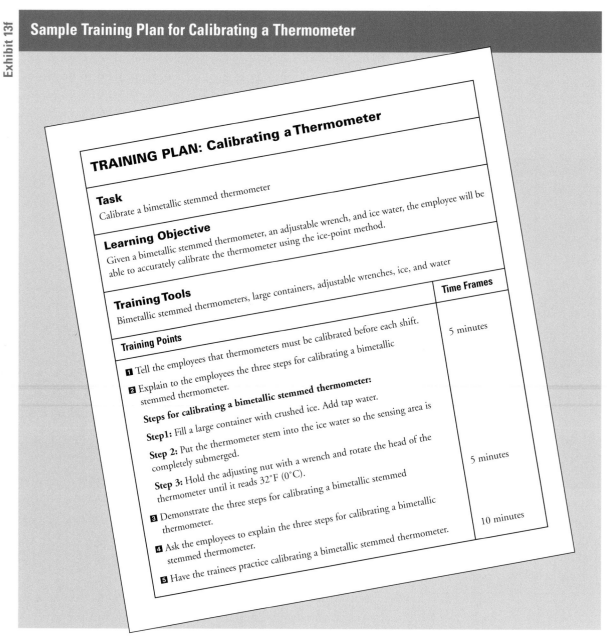

TRAINING PLAN: Calibrating a Thermometer

Task
Calibrate a bimetallic stemmed thermometer

Learning Objective
Given a bimetallic stemmed thermometer, an adjustable wrench, and ice water, the employee will be able to accurately calibrate the thermometer using the ice-point method.

Training Tools
Bimetallic stemmed thermometers, large containers, adjustable wrenches, ice, and water

Training Points	Time Frames
1 Tell the employees that thermometers must be calibrated before each shift.	5 minutes
2 Explain to the employees the three steps for calibrating a bimetallic stemmed thermometer.	
Steps for calibrating a bimetallic stemmed thermometer:	
Step1: Fill a large container with crushed ice. Add tap water.	
Step 2: Put the thermometer stem into the ice water so the sensing area is completely submerged.	
Step 3: Hold the adjusting nut with a wrench and rotate the head of the thermometer until it reads 32°F (0°C).	5 minutes
3 Demonstrate the three steps for calibrating a bimetallic thermometer.	
4 Ask the employees to explain the three steps for calibrating a bimetallic stemmed thermometer.	10 minutes
5 Have the trainees practice calibrating a bimetallic stemmed thermometer.	

A training plan should include learning objectives, training tools, and a list of specific training points that will be covered.

Practice

Two-thirds of the time spent training should be devoted to activities that allow employees to apply what they have learned and receive feedback.

Guidelines for Effective Training

There are several things you can do when delivering training to make it easier for your employees to learn:

- **Prepare for the presentation.** Make sure you are knowledgeable in all areas of food safety. Practice the presentation using your training plan and rehearse until it feels natural.

- **Help employees see "what's in it for me."** To get employees attention, you must show them how the training will help them do their jobs faster, easier, or better.

- **Let employees practice and apply information.** As a general rule, one-third of the time spent training should be devoted to presenting content. The remaining two-thirds should be devoted to activities that allow employees to apply what they have learned and receive feedback. (See *Exhibit 13g.*) Application or practice without feedback will be ineffective. Feedback must be specific, immediate, and worded positively. It should also be given for both correct and incorrect performance.

- **Follow a logical sequence when presenting information.** Information should be presented step by step from start to finish.

- **Tie new knowledge to past knowledge when presenting information.** Build on employees' past knowledge and experiences.

- **Present information using the "zoom" principle.** Think in terms of a zoom lens on a camera. Begin by zooming out—explaining the big picture to employees. This is a high-level overview of the information you are presenting. Next, "zoom" in on some detail, and then back out to the big picture before covering the next detail.

- **Present information in "chunks."** Break lessons down into smaller, more manageable pieces of information. Allow employees to practice each chunk until they have mastered it. Do not teach the next chunk until they have mastered the previous one. Each piece of information should cover between five to nine major points.

■ **Keep training sessions short.** The ideal length is probably twenty to thirty minutes. Longer sessions can be effective if they are well planned and incorporate a variety of learning activities.

■ **Wrap up the training session properly.** Give an overview of what was covered during the session, highlighting important information. Employees should be able to answer questions about the material. They should also be able to properly demonstrate tasks they practiced during the training session. Remind employees why the information they learned is important.

Apply Your Knowledge	**Rule of Thumb**
Fill in the blanks.	You have ninety minutes to present a lesson on food safety in your establishment. To be effective, ___ minutes should be spent actually presenting the lesson, while ___ minutes should be spent allowing participants to apply the information they have learned, with feedback. **For answers, please turn to page 13-23.**

Training Delivery Methods

Training can be delivered using a variety of methods. Some establishments opt for a more traditional approach, using lecture, demonstration, or role-play in either a one-on-one or group format. Others use technology to deliver training. No single method of delivery is best for all employees because each learns differently. Using several methods will result in more effective learning. The delivery methods you choose should allow employees to:

■ Reflect on content and determine how it applies to their job

■ Talk to each other about content

■ See tasks being performed and perform the tasks themselves

■ Hear instructions

■ Read materials and take notes

■ Reason through real-life situations

One-On-One Training

Many establishments deliver food safety training to employees on a one-on-one basis. This method has many advantages and is often preferred because it:

- Takes into consideration the needs of individual employees (see *Exhibit 13h*)

- Can take place on the job, thus eliminating the need for a separate training location

- Enables the manager to monitor employee progress

- Allows for immediate feedback

- Offers the opportunity to apply information that has been learned

One-on-one training does have some disadvantages, however. Most important, its effectiveness depends upon the ability of the person delivering the training. Therefore, the trainer must be selected very carefully. Many establishments certify trainers or validate that they have the appropriate skills before allowing them to train.

Group Training

If several employees require food safety training, group sessions might be a more practical way to deliver it. When training is delivered this way:

- It is more cost effective.

- Training is more uniform.

- You know precisely what employees have been taught.

As with one-one-one training, the effectiveness of group training depends upon the skill and ability of the trainer. It can also be a challenge to deliver training this way since employees may bring a mix of learning styles to the session. Additionally, group training often does not take into account the needs of the individual learner. Slower learners, less-skilled employees, or those with limited proficiency in English may not understand all the material presented.

Exhibit 13h

One-on-One Training

One advantage of one-on-one training is that it takes into consideration the needs of individual employees.

Trainers must remember to keep employees involved during the training session. If involved, they will have a greater chance of retaining information. Studies on training effectiveness show that trainees retain:

- Ten percent of what they read

- Twenty percent of what they hear

- Thirty percent of what they see

- Fifty percent of what they hear and see

- Seventy percent of what they say

- Ninety percent of what they say and do

Lecture

A lecture is a prepared oral presentation used to deliver content to a group of participants. Lectures are most effective when mixed with other presentation methods and media, and are better received and accepted when the following techniques are used:

- Start with an interesting statement, observation, quotation, or question.

- Use relevant humor where appropriate.

- Use interesting and relevant examples, anecdotes, analogies, and statistics.

- Ask frequent questions to solicit audience participation.

- Use frequent small-group discussions and activities.

- Build in a review.

Demonstration

Many times you may be required to teach specific food safety tasks by demonstrating them to a person or group. Demonstrations will be most effective if you follow the "Tell/Show/Tell/Show" model. (See *Exhibit 13i.*)

Exhibit 13i

Demonstrating a Task Using the Tell/Show/Tell/Show Model

1 Tell them how to do it.

Explain the overall steps using written procedures, diagrams, forms, etc.

2 Show them how to do it.

Demonstrate the task slowly, so employees can see what is happening. Then repeat the demonstration at normal speed.

Emphasize key points as you demonstrate the task. Explain how each step fits into the task sequence.

3 Have them tell you how to do it.

Ask employees to explain each of the steps in sequence.

4 Have them show you how to do it.

Ask employees to demonstrate the task. Provide appropriate feedback, correcting errors as they occur.

Role-Play

In role-plays, trainees act out a situation to try out new skills or apply what has been learned. They usually are set up so one employee is confronted by another employee and must answer questions, handle problems, provide satisfaction, solve a complaint, etc. Different types of role-plays are suitable for different types of learning situations. For example, a role-play can be used to teach a manager how to work with a health inspector during an inspection. When using a role-play, you should:

- Keep the role-play simple.

- Provide employees with detailed instructions.

- Explain and model the situation before employees begin.

Exhibit 13j

Job Aids

Job aids can be used to train employees and provide a reference while back on the job.

Job Aids

Job aids can also be used to train employees. They include worksheets, checklists, flowcharts, written procedures, glossaries, diagrams, decision tables, etc. Posters that illustrate the steps for proper handwashing, or washing dishes in a three-compartment sink are good examples. (See *Exhibit 13j*.) Job aids have the added benefit of serving as a reference for employees while on the job. They are particularly useful when:

- Consequences of making a mistake are severe.

- Safety is a concern.

- Tasks are performed infrequently.

- Tasks are complex.

- Sequence is critical when performing the task.

Training Videos and DVDs

Training videos and DVDs can be used to introduce information, reinforce information during the session, or review information at the end of the training session. They can be great tools if used properly. However, they will be much less effective if they are simply played for employees without your direct involvement. To use videos and DVDs effectively, you should:

- Familiarize yourself with the content.

- Prepare employees by explaining what they will learn and why it is important.

- Select stopping points to discuss concepts or practices that require emphasis.

- Ask questions afterward to reinforce content.

Exhibit 13k

Technology-Based Training

Web-based training and interactive CD-ROMs provide consistent training delivery and feedback.

Technology-Based Training

Web-based training, interactive CD-ROMs, and other technology-based training programs offer yet another way to deliver training. The benefits of technology-based training include:

- **Consistent delivery and feedback.** (See *Exhibit 13k.*) The training and feedback are delivered the same way every time.

- **Learner control.** Employees may have control over their learning path.

- **Interactive instruction.** Employees are able to interact, review, and explore the content.

- **Increased practice.** Employees are allowed to practice a skill until they are proficient.

- **Self-paced training.** Employees can progress at their own pace.

- **Training records are easily created and stored.** Technology-based training can automatically track an individual's training progress and exam scores. Accessing this information and generating the necessary reports is often very easy.

- **Training can be delivered anytime, anywhere.** Web-based training is available anytime and anywhere there is an Internet connection.

- **Reduced cost.** Technology-based training can reduce training costs by freeing up trainers and eliminating travel costs.

- **Training that engages and supports different learning styles.** Technology-based training can be very engaging since it often includes a variety of media, such as video, sound, animation, photos, etc. For this reason, it often works well for the visual and auditory learner.

- **Multilingual training.** The training can be delivered in more than one language.

Games

Games can be used to create excitement and get employees' attention when the material is difficult or mundane. Games can also be used to practice previously learned principles. (See *Exhibit 13l*.) Games should be short, simple, and provide some type of reward. To use games effectively, you should:

- Explain how they relate to the information being presented.

- Explain the rules carefully.

- Have a practice round before actually playing the game.

- Make sure employees do not lose sight of the game's purpose while playing.

- Discuss the game after it has finished.

Case Studies

Case studies are a good way to let employees apply what they have learned. By this method, employees are presented with a fictional or real-world story that poses specific problems. They are then asked to apply what they have learned to solve them.

Exhibit 13l

Games

Games can be used to practice principles learned in the training session and create excitement.

The trainer provides feedback on how employees dealt with the problems and discusses other ways they might have been handled. When conducting case studies:

■ Provide clear instructions.

■ Make sure employees see the case study's relevance.

■ Make sure employees identify realistic solution(s).

■ Carefully facilitate the discussion.

Apply Your Knowledge

Read each statement and determine the training delivery method it represents by placing the letter of the method in the space provided.

There's More than One Way to Skin a Cat!

____ **1** Often allows employees to choose their own learning path when receiving food safety training

____ **2** Requires employees to find a solution to a food safety problem posed by a fictional or real-world story

____ **3** Requires employees to act out a food safety situation to apply what they learned

____ **4** Can be used to teach food safety concepts and serves as a reference when employees get back on the job

____ **5** Requires employees to first explain how a food safety task should be performed prior to actually performing the task

____ **6** Not as effective for teaching food safety concepts unless stopping points are selected to discuss them

____ **7** Creates excitement by allowing employees to compete against each other

A. Demonstration

B. Game

C. Videos and DVDs

D. Case study

E. Job aid

F. Role-play

G. Web-based training and interactive CD-ROMs

For answers, please turn to page 13-23.

Exhibit 13m

Using Appropriate Training Materials

If employees are not proficient in English, use training materials translated into their native language.

Selecting Training Materials

Training materials help participants learn and retain information, add interest, save time, and make the trainer's job easier. To be useful, they must be:

- **Accurate.** Materials must be factual, up-to-date, and complete. To ensure they are accurate, food safety training materials should be based upon the latest in the science of food safety. Sources for information should include recognized authorities from associations, universities, or federal, state and local health departments. To ensure that materials are relevant, they should also be based upon best practices in the industry.

  Regulatory requirements or guidance documents can be used to deliver food safety training. Materials can also be developed internally, or purchased from professional or educational organizations, industry suppliers, or other authorities in foodservice training.

- **Appropriate.** Written materials must be matched to the reading-comprehension levels of employees. For employees with limited English proficiency, training materials in other languages should be used. (See *Exhibit 13m.*) In addition, materials should suit the abilities of the trainer. Limitations imposed by the training location will influence your choice of training materials. For example, in order to use technology-based tools, the proper equipment must be available.

- **Attractive.** When teaching subjects that generally do not have a wide appeal, it is critical that you hold the employees' attention. To do this, create eye-catching training materials. Design the information to be memorable, and make sure the materials involve the employees by providing meaningful activities.

TRAINING FOLLOW-UP

It is critical to follow up with employees after the training session has ended. By doing so, you can determine whether or not they can still do what they were trained to do. Proper follow-up can also help ensure training will have a lasting effect. You can follow up with employees by:

- Giving periodic quizzes to test their knowledge of the learned material

- Periodically asking them to demonstrate the new tasks they have learned

- Comparing on-the-job performance to company policy

Follow-up should occur within thirty days of the training session. Research suggests that after thirty days, there is less of a chance that employees will retain the information learned.

FOOD SAFETY CERTIFICATION

The National Restaurant Association and federal and state regulatory officials recommend food safety training and certification, particularly for managers and supervisors. Certification demonstrates that a person comprehends basic food safety principles and recommended food safety practices that prevent foodborne illness.

Manager certification is already a requirement in some states. In other states, some cities and counties require certification, although the state as a whole does not require it. The National Restaurant Association Educational Foundation Web site provides a jurisdictional summary of training and certification requirements for the entire country.

Regardless of state regulations, many proactive establishments and managers have made a strong commitment to food safety training. You should make the same commitment to training, as well as certification even if your city or state does not require it. As a conscientious restaurant or foodservice manager, you should train your employees, monitor their practices, and make food safety a part of everyone's job description. In this way, you will be able to ensure that the food you serve is safe.

SUMMARY

As a manager, it is your responsibility to ensure that employees have the knowledge and skills needed to handle food safely in your establishment. Some of the benefits can include preventing a foodborne-illness outbreak, avoiding the loss of revenue and reputation following an outbreak, improving employee morale, and increasing customer satisfaction.

Your first task is to assess the training needs in your establishment. A training need is a gap between what employees are required to know to perform their jobs and what they actually know. To identify food safety training needs, you can test your employees' knowledge, observe their performance, or survey them to identify areas of weakness.

All employees require general food safety knowledge. Other knowledge will be specific to the tasks performed on the job. From their first day, new employees should receive training on the importance of food safety, proper personal hygiene, and safe food preparation practices. They should also receive training on proper cleaning and sanitizing practices, safe chemical handling, and pest prevention.

Regardless of their position, employees need to be retrained periodically. This can be accomplished by scheduling short retraining sessions, holding meetings to update staff on new procedures, or conducting motivational sessions that reinforce food safety practices. Keep records of all training conducted at your establishment. For legal reasons, it is important to document that employees have completed food safety training.

A successful food safety training program will be led by clearly defined and measurable objectives. Training must support these objectives, and there must be methods for evaluating the training to ensure objectives have been met. True success cannot be achieved unless the work climate supports the training, and it has management support.

Before any training actually occurs, you should begin with the necessary planning. This includes choosing appropriate training delivery methods, selecting training materials, and determining the best method for evaluating employee knowledge after the session. Planning also includes making administrative decisions such as where to hold the training, and how to schedule it. Once these decisions have been made, the next step is to create an agenda or training plan.

Training can be delivered using a variety of methods. Some establishments use technology to deliver it. Others opt for a more traditional approach, including lecture, demonstration, or role-play methods—either one-on-one or in a group training format. No single method of delivery is best for all employees because each learns differently. Using several methods will result in more effective learning.

Following up with employees within thirty days of the training session is critical in determining if employees can still do what they were trained to do. Follow up by giving periodic quizzes, asking employees to demonstrate the new tasks they learned, and by comparing on-the-job performance to company policy.

The National Restaurant Association and federal and state regulatory officials recommend food safety training and certification, particularly for managers. Certification shows that a person comprehends basic food safety principles and recommended food safety practices that prevent foodborne illnesses.

Apply Your Knowledge

Use these questions to test your knowledge of the concepts presented in this section.

Multiple-Choice Study Questions

1. Which is true regarding food safety training?

   A. The ideal length for a training session is one to two hours.

   B. Training records should be used to document training.

   C. Employees only require food safety knowledge that is specific to their job tasks.

   D. Further training is unnecessary if employees received training upon being hired.

2. New employees should receive training on

   A. HACCP.

   B. crisis management.

   C. active managerial control.

   D. pest identification and prevention.

3. Which is true about group training?

   A. It ensures that training is more uniform.

   B. It allows employees to learn at their own pace.

   C. It allows employees to choose their own learning path.

   A. It is better able to meet the needs of the individual learner.

4. When demonstrating a task, you should do all of these *except*

   A. explain task steps before demonstrating them.

   B. demonstrate the task and then explain what was demonstrated.

   C. have the employee explain the steps before demonstrating them.

   D. demonstrate the task slowly the first time and then again at normal speed.

5. Which is true when delivering food safety training?

   A. The lecture method should always be used to deliver it.

   B. A Web-based method should always be used to deliver it.

   C. To prevent confusion, do not use more than one method of delivery.

   D. Use several delivery methods because each employee learns differently.

For answers, please turn to page 13-23.

Apply Your Knowledge   Answers

Page	Activity

13-2   Test Your Food Safety Knowledge

1. True   2. False   3. False   4. True   5. True

13-10   Rule of Thumb

30, 60

13-17   There's More than One Way to Skin a Cat!

1. G   3. F   5. A   7. B

2. D   4. E   6. C

13-22   Multiple-Choice Study Questions

1. B   2. D   3. A   4. B   5. D

Appendix

HOW TO IMPLEMENT THE FOOD SAFETY PRACTICES LEARNED IN THE SERVSAFE PROGRAM

The ServSafe program will provide you with the essential knowledge to help keep food safe in your establishment. It is your responsibility to implement that knowledge. To do this, you must examine the following aspects of your operation and compare them to your newfound ServSafe knowledge:

■ Current food safety policies and procedures

■ Employee training

■ Your facilities

The steps listed below will help you make the comparison that will take you from where you are today to where you need to be to *consistently* keep food safe in your establishment:

1 Evaluate your current food safety practices using the Food Safety Evaluation Checklist located in this Appendix. This checklist, which begins on page A-3, identifies the most critical food safety practices that must be followed in every operation. It consists of a series of Yes/No questions that will assist you in identifying opportunities for improvement. Wherever a *No* is checked in this evaluation, you have identified a gap in your food safety practices. These gaps will be the starting point for improving your current food safety program.

2 **Review the "How This Relates to Me" areas located throughout the text in** *ServSafe Essentials.* These are the write-in areas in the text that capture specific food safety requirements in your jurisdiction. If a requirement differs from your company policy or is not addressed by it, you have identified a gap in your food safety program and an opportunity for improvement.

3 **Determine the cause of the gaps identified in Steps 1 and 2.** For example, if you find that your walk-in cooler is incapable of holding food at 41°F (5°C) or lower, you have identified a gap. There are many things that could have caused this situation, including faulty equipment, a walk-in door that is opened too frequently, etc. You must explore each of these potential causes to determine the true reason for the gap.

4 **Create a solution that addresses the gaps.** This may include:

- Developing or revising Standard Operating Procedures (SOPs)

- Training employees on new or revised SOPs

- Implementing SOPs

- Bringing existing equipment up to standard or purchasing new equipment

- Training or retraining employees

5 **Evaluate your solution periodically to ensure it has addressed the gaps identified in Steps 1 and 2.**

FOOD SAFETY SELF ASSESSMENT

The following self assessment (pages A-3 through A-11) not only helps you identify food safety gaps in your establishment, but can also help you implement food safety systems such as active managerial control. This self assessment—the Food Safety Evaluation Checklist—can help you address the five risk factors identified by the Centers for Disease Control and Prevention (CDC) as well as other food safety risks in your establishment. Use this tool to identify gaps and areas to develop SOPs, policies, and meaningful food safety programs. Once you are finished, you can prioritize your gaps and work on creating a solution.

Directions: Check *Yes* after each question if your establishment currently performs the practice or *No* if it currently does not. Each practice that is checked *No* identifies a gap that offers an opportunity for revising your food safety program.

Food Safety Evaluation Checklist

Topic/Principle	Evaluation	Page Reference in *Essentials*
Failing to Cook Food Adequately; Holding Food at Improper Temperatures		
1. Are time and temperature controls part of every employee's job?	Yes _____ No _____	5-6
2. Are time and temperature controls incorporated in your SOPs?	Yes _____ No _____	5-7
3. Are calibrated thermometers available to all foodhandlers?	Yes _____ No _____	5-6
4. Do you calibrate thermometers regularly?	Yes _____ No _____	5-12
5. Do all employees know how to properly use thermometers?	Yes _____ No _____	5-10 through 5-13
6. Do you minimize the amount of time food spends in the temperature danger zone (41°F [5°C] to 135°F [57°C])?	Yes _____ No _____	5-5
7. Do you document product temperatures in a temperature log or line check?	Yes _____ No _____	5-6
8. Do you reject food that has *not* been received at the proper temperature?	Yes _____ No _____	6-5 through 6-19

Continued on next page…

Food Safety Evaluation Checklist *continued*

Topic/Principle	Evaluation	Page Reference in *Essentials*
Failing to Cook Food Adequately; Holding Food at Improper Temperatures *continued*		
9. Do you store potentially hazardous food at its required storage temperature?	Yes ____ No ____	7-9 through 7-11
10. Do you properly thaw food?	Yes ____ No ____	8-3
11. Do you cook potentially hazardous food to the the required minimum internal temperatures?	Yes ____ No ____	8-8 through 8-13
12. Do you cool cooked, potentially hazardous food according to the required time and temperature requirements?	Yes ____ No ____	8-15
13. Do you reheat potentially hazardous food that will be hot held to 165°F (74°C) for fifteen seconds within two hours?	Yes ____ No ____	8-18
14. Do you hold potentially hazardous food at the proper temperature (41°F [5°C] or lower, or 135°F [57°C] or higher)?	Yes ____ No ____	9-3 through 9-4
Protecting Food and Equipment from Contamination		
1. Are your handwashing stations equipped with the necessary tools and supplies?	Yes ____ No ____	11-10 through 11-11
2. Is the equipment you purchase designed with sanitation in mind?	Yes ____ No ____	11-12 through 11-13
3. Do your employees store cleaning cloths in a sanitizer solution between uses?	Yes ____ No ____	11-30
4. Do your employees know the frequency for cleaning and sanitizing food-contact surfaces?	Yes ____ No ____	11-22

Food Safety Evaluation Checklist

Topic/Principle	Evaluation	Page Reference in *Essentials*

Protecting Food and Equipment from Contamination *continued*

Topic/Principle	Evaluation	Page Reference in *Essentials*
5. Do your employees know how to effectively use the sanitizer in your establishment?	Yes _____ No _____	11-25
6. Do your dishwashing employees know how to properly use the dishwashing machine?	Yes _____ No _____	11-26 through 11-28
7. Do your dishwashing employees know how to properly clean and sanitize items in a three-compartment sink?	Yes _____ No _____	11-28 through 11-29
8. Do your employees know how to properly clean and sanitize stationary equipment?	Yes _____ No _____	11-30 through 11-31
9. Do your employees know how to clean nonfood-contact surfaces?	Yes _____ No _____	11-31 through 11-32
10. Do your employees know how to properly store clean and sanitized utensils, tableware, and equipment?	Yes _____ No _____	11-33 through 11-34
11. Do you have a master cleaning program in place?	Yes _____ No _____	11-36 through 11-37
12. Do you store food in a way that prevents contamination?		
A. Do you store food in designated storage areas only?	Yes _____ No _____	7-4
B. Do you store cooked or ready-to-eat food above raw meat, poultry, and fish?	Yes _____ No _____	7-6
C. Do you store dry food away from walls and at least six inches off the floor?	Yes _____ No _____	7-8

Continued on next page…

Food Safety Evaluation Checklist *continued*

Topic/Principle	Evaluation	Page Reference in *Essentials*
Protecting Food and Equipment from Contamination *continued*		
13. Do you prepare food in a way that prevents contamination?		
A. Is the work flow of your establishment designed for food safety?	Yes _____ No _____	11-5
B. Do you assign specific equipment to each type of food product used in your establishment?	Yes _____ No _____	5-4
C. Do you clean and sanitize all work surfaces, equipment, and utensils after each task?	Yes _____ No _____	5-4
D. When using the same prep table to prepare food, do you prepare raw and ready-to-eat food at different times?	Yes _____ No _____	5-4
E. Do you use ingredients that require minimal preparation?	Yes _____ No _____	5-4
14. Do you hold food in a way that prevents contamination?		
A. Do you shield or cover food to protect it from contamination?	Yes _____ No _____	9-4
B. Do you discard food being held for service after a predetermined amount of time?	Yes _____ No _____	9-3
15. Do you serve food in a way that prevents contamination?		
A. Do you minimize bare-hand contact with food that is cooked or ready to eat?	Yes _____ No _____	9-7
B. Do servers avoid handling the food-contact surfaces of glassware, dishes, and utensils?	Yes _____ No _____	9-8
C. Do you maintain self-service areas in a way that prevents contamination?	Yes _____ No _____	9-11

Food Safety Evaluation Checklist

Topic/Principle	Evaluation	Page Reference in *Essentials*
Protecting Food and Equipment from Contamination *continued*		
16. Do you handle chemicals in a way that prevents contamination?		
A. Do you store chemicals away from food, utensils, and equipment?	Yes _____ No _____	3-15
B. Are containers used to dispense chemicals properly labeled?	Yes _____ No _____	3-15
C. If pesticides are applied in the establishment, are all food and food-contact surfaces removed prior to the application?	Yes _____ No _____	11-45
17. Do you only use food-grade utensils in your establishment?	Yes _____ No _____	3-15
18. Is your lighting installed in a manner that prohibits food contamination?	Yes _____ No _____	11-20
Using Approved Sources		
1. Do you purchase food from suppliers that obtain their products from approved sources?	Yes _____ No _____	6-3
2. Do you ensure that your suppliers are reputable?	Yes _____ No _____	6-3
3. Do your suppliers deliver during off-peak hours?	Yes _____ No _____	6-3

Continued on next page...

Food Safety Evaluation Checklist *continued*

Topic/Principle	Evaluation	Page Reference in *Essentials*
Proper Personal Hygiene		
1. Are all employees aware of all the ways in which they can contaminate food?	Yes _____ No _____	4-3 through 4-4
2. Do all employees follow the proper procedure for handwashing?	Yes _____ No _____	4-7
3. Are all employees aware of the instances when handwashing is required?	Yes _____ No _____	4-6
4. Do all employees follow the proper hand maintenance procedures, such as keeping nails short and clean, and covering cuts and sores?	Yes _____ No _____	4-8
5. Do you provide the right type of gloves in your establishment for handling food?	Yes _____ No _____	4-10 through 4-11
6. Do employees change gloves when necessary?	Yes _____ No _____	4-11
7. Do you have requirements for proper work attire for foodhandlers?	Yes _____ No _____	4-12
8. Do you require employees to maintain personal cleanliness?	Yes _____ No _____	4-12
9. Do you prohibit employees from smoking, eating, or drinking in food preparation and dishwashing areas?	Yes _____ No _____	4-13
10. Do you have policies to address employee illnesses and injury?	Yes _____ No _____	4-14
11. Do you model proper foodhandling behaviors at all times?	Yes _____ No _____	4-16

Food Safety Evaluation Checklist

Topic/Principle	Evaluation	Page Reference in *Essentials*
Facilities and Equipment		
1. Is stationary food equipment installed properly?	Yes _____ No _____	11-14 through 11-15
2. Does your food equipment receive regular maintenance?	Yes _____ No _____	11-16
3. Is your plumbing installed and maintained by a licensed plumber?	Yes _____ No _____	11-17
4. Is lighting set at intensities required to ensure food safety?	Yes _____ No _____	11-19
5. Is garbage properly removed from the premises?	Yes _____ No _____	11-21
Pest Control		
1. Do you have a contract with a licensed pest control operator?	Yes _____ No _____	11-38
2. Do you inspect deliveries for signs of pests?	Yes _____ No _____	11-39
3. Do you take measures for preventing pests from entering the establishment?	Yes _____ No _____	11-39 through 11-40
4. Do you take measures for denying pests food and shelter in the establishment?	Yes _____ No _____	11-40 through 11-42
5. Can your employees identify signs of pests?	Yes _____ No _____	11-42 through 11-43

Continued on next page...

Food Safety Evaluation Checklist *continued*

Topic/Principle	Evaluation	Page Reference in *Essentials*
Food Safety Systems		
1. Do you have the necessary prerequisite programs for a food safety system in place?	Yes _____ No _____	10-3
2. Does your food safety management system focus on controlling the five most common risk factors responsible for foodborne illness as identified by the CDC?	Yes _____ No _____	10-3
3. Does your food safety management system focus on identifying, monitoring, and controlling significant biological, chemical, and physical hazards?	Yes _____ No _____	3-3
4. Do you know when a Hazard Analysis Critical Control Point (HACCP) plan is required?	Yes _____ No _____	10-11 through 10-12
Employee Training		
1. Do you have food safety training programs for both new and current employees?	Yes _____ No _____	13-4
2. Do you have assessment tools that identify food safety training needs for employees?	Yes _____ No _____	13-4
3. Do you have a variety of food safety training resources that include books, videos, posters, and technology-based materials to meet your employees' learning needs?	Yes _____ No _____	13-10
4. Do you keep records documenting that employees have completed training?	Yes _____ No _____	13-4

Food Safety Evaluation Checklist

Topic/Principle	Evaluation	Page Reference in *Essentials*
Auditing (Self Inspection)		
1. Do you conduct regular self inspections?	Yes _____ No _____	12-5
2. Do you regularly compare your local or state sanitation regulations to procedures at your establishment?	Yes _____ No _____	12-12
3. Are all infractions from regulatory or self inspections addressed in a timely manner?	Yes _____ No _____	12-8 through 12-9
4. Do you have a plan for working with health inspectors during inspections?	Yes _____ No _____	12-8 through 12-9

Index

A

acidity, 2-5
Acquired Immune Deficiency
    Syndrome (AIDS), 4-4
air gap, 11-3, 11-18
air quality, 11-20
allergen, 3-3, 3-19 thru 3-20, 10-7
Americans with Disabilities Act
    (*see* government regulations
    and regulatory agencies)
Amnesic Shellfish Poisoning (ASP),
    3-12
Anisakiasis *(Anisakis simplex)*, 2-29
antiseptic, 4-6
approved food source, 6-3, 10-4
aseptically packaged food, 6-18
    receiving criteria, 6-18
attire, 4-12
automatic shutoff controls, 9-14

B

backflow, 11-3, 11-17, 11-18
bacteria, 2-2, 2-6, 2-8, 2-9, 6-14, 7-7,
    8-7, 10-7, 10-10
    bacterial illness, 2-9 thru 2-21
bakery goods, 6-19
    receiving criteria, 6-19
bandage, 4-9, 4-14

bare-hand contact, 4-8, 9-7, 9-8
batter and breading, 8-5 thru 8-6
beef, 2-21
blast chiller, 8-16
bleach, 11-25
Botulism *(Clostridium botulinum)*,
    2-19
buffet, 9-11
building code, 11-19

C

Campylobacteriosis
    (Campylobacter jejuni), 2-11
canned food, 6-16, 7-11
    receiving criteria, 6-16
    storage requirements, 7-11
carbonated-beverage dispenser, 3-15
carrier, 4-2, 4-4
Centers for Disease Control
    and Prevention (CDC)
    (*see* government regulations
    and regulatory agencies)
certificate of operation, 11-7
    suspension of, 12-10 thru 12-11
cheese, 2-34
chemicals, 3-15, 3-16
ciguatera fish poisoning, 3-3, 3-7
cleaning, 5-4, 9-8, 11-4,
    11-21 thru 11-37, 11-41

employee, 3-19 thru 3-20,
    4-3 thru 4-16, 5-6, 9-6 thru 9-11,
    10-14, 11-36, 11-37, 11-41, 12-8,
    12-10, 13-2 thru 13-19
    employee illness and injury,
        4-14, 4-15
    training, 11-37, 12-10,
        13-2 thru 13-19
Environmental Protection Agency
    (EPA) (see government
    regulations and regulatory
    agencies)
equipment, 5-4, 11-6, 10-3, 10-8,
    11-12 thru 11-16
    clean-in-place equipment, 11-14
    cleaning and sanitizing,
        11-30 thru 11-31
    portable equipment, 11-15
    sanitation standards,
        11-12 thru 11-14
    stationary equipment, 11-15,
        11-30 thru 11-31
    storage, 11-33 thru 11-34
exclusion, 4-2
expiration date, 7-3, 7-4, 9-14

F

FAT TOM, 2-3, 2-5
FDA (see government regulations
    and regulatory agencies)
feedback, 10-4
finger cot, 4-2, 4-9
first-in, first-out method (FIFO)
    (see product rotation)
fish, 2-29, 3-4 thru 3-7, 6-6 thru 6-7,
    7-9, 8-4, 8-12
    cooking requirements, 8-12
    preparation, 8-4
    receiving criteria, 6-6
    storage requirements, 7-9
flooring, 11-8 thru 11-10
    carpeting, 11-9
    hard-surface flooring, 11-9
    nonporous resilient flooring,
        11-8 thru 11-9

porosity, 11-8
special flooring needs, 11-10
    coving, 11-10
    nonslip surface, 11-10
    rubber mat, 11-10
flow of food, 1-2, 5-2 thru 5-13,
    6-2 thru 6-20, 7-2 thru 7-11,
    8-2 thru 8-18, 9-2 thru 9-14, 12-6
food allergy, 3-3, 3-19 thru 3-20
food bar, 9-11
Food and Drug Administration
    (FDA) (see government
    regulations and regulatory
    agencies)
food preparation, 8-2 thru 8-18
food safety, 1-2 thru 1-10,
    2-1 thru 2-34, 3-2 thru 3-20,
    4-2 thru 4-16, 5-2 thru 5-13,
    6-2 thru 6-20, 7-2 thru 7-11,
    8-2 thru 8-18, 9-2 thru 9-14,
    10-2 thru 10-17, 11-36,
    12-2 thru 12-12, 13-4, 13-19
    active managerial control,
        10-2 thru 10-4
    certification, 13-19
    crisis management,
        10-12 thru 10-17
    food safety knowledge,
        13-4, 13-5
    HACCP system, 10-2,
        10-5 thru 10-11
    management system,
        10-2 thru 10-17
    monitoring, 10-4
    policies and procedures, 10-4
    potential hazards, 1-8, 10-5, 10-7
        biological, 1-8
        chemical, 1-8
        physical, 1-8
    prerequisite food safety
        programs, 10-3, 10-5
    regulations and standards,
        12-2 thru 12-12
    risk factors, 10-4
    training, 13-2 thru 13-19

Food Safety and Inspection Service
    (FSIS) (see government
    regulations and regulatory
    agencies)
food security, 3-2, 3-17 thru 3-19
food shield, 9-11
foodborne illness, 1-2 thru 1-10 ,
    2-4 thru 2-32, 3-4 thru 3-14, 4-3,
    5-5, 8-3, 8-4, 8-9, 10-11, 10-12,
    10-14, 10-16, 10-17, 11-17, 12-7, 13-3
    classification of, 2-7
    costs of, 1-4, 1-5, 13-3
    foodborne illness outbreak,
        1-2, 8-4, 10-12, 10-17, 11-17,
        12-10, 13-3
    prevention of, 1-4 thru 1-8
foodborne infection, 2-4, 2-7, 2-9,
    2-11 thru 2-16
foodborne intoxication, 2-4, 2-7
    thru 2-9, 2-17 thru 2-19
foodborne toxin-mediated
    infection, 2-4, 2-8, 2-9,
    2-20 thru 2-21
foodhandling, 1-9, 4-3 thru 4-16,
    9-2 thru 9-14, 12-10, 13-7
freezing, 2-7, 6-6 thru 6-7,
    7-7 thru 7-8, 8-3
frozen processed food, 6-14
    receiving criteria, 6-14
frozen yogurt, 7-10
    storage requirements, 7-10
fungi, 2-3, 2-34

G

garbage, 11-21, 11-40
    container, 11-21
    disposal of, 11-21, 11-40
gastroenteritis,
    (Bacillus cereus), 2-17
    (Clostridium perfringens), 2-20
    Norovirus, 2-26
    staphylococcal (Staphylococcus
        aureus), 2-18, 4-4
    (Vibrio parahaemolyticus), 2-15
    (Vibrio vulnificus), 2-16

I

ice, 8-8, 9-8
    preparation, 8-8
ice cream, 7-10
    storage requirements, 7-10
icepaddle, 8-3, 8-16
ice-water bath, 8-3, 8-16
incentive, 11-37
infected lesion, 4-2, 4-3
infestation, 11-4
insulated container, 9-12, 9-13
integrated pest management
    program (IPM), 11-4,
    11-38 thru 11-42
    denying access, 11-38 thru 11-40
        deliveries, 11-39
        doors, windows, vents, 11-39
        floors and walls, 11-40
        pipes, 11-39
    denying food and shelter, 11-38,
        11-40 thru 11-41
    elimination, 11-38,
        11-42 thru 11-45
internal temperature
    (*see* temperature)
Interstate Certified Shellfish
    Shippers List, 6-8

J

jaundice, 4-3
jewelry, 4-12, 13-7
juice, 8-7
    preparation, 8-7

K

kitchen, 11-5, 11-6
    equipment maintenance,
        11-14, 11-16
    installation of equipment,
        11-14, 11-15

kitchen layout, 11-5 thru 11-6
    contamination, 11-6
    equipment accessibility, 11-6
    workflow, 11-5
kitchen staff, 9-6 thru 9-7

L

labeling, 7-3, 7-4, 7-8, 9-5, 9-11, 9-13
leftovers, 8-4, 9-13
lighting, 11-19 thru 11-20
    foot-candle, 11-19
listeriosis *(Listeria
    monocytogenes)*, 2-14, 6-11

M

manager, 3-18, 4-6, 4-16, 10-3
    thru 10-4, 12-8, 13-4, 13-7, 13-19
    certification, 13-19
master cleaning schedule, 11-4,
    11-36, 12-10
Material Safety Data Sheet
    (MSDS), 11-4, 11-35, 11-36, 11-45
meat, 6-5, 7-9, 8-4, 8-11 thru 8-12
    cooking requirements,
        8-11 thru 8-12
    preparation, 8-4
    receiving criteria, 6-5
    storage requirements, 7-9
medication, 4-14
microorganism, 1-6, 1-8, 1-9,
    2-2, 2-4 thru 2-34, 4-3, 4-4,
    5-3 thru 5-4, 6-18, 8-3 thru 8-5,
    8-8, 8-9, 8-15
    controlling growth of, 2-6, 2-7
    growth of, 2-5, 2-6 thru 2-7
    spoilage microorganism, 2-4
microwave, 8-11

modified atmosphere packaging
    (MAP), 6-2, 6-15
moisture, 2-6
mold, 2-3, 2-4, 2-34
mushrooms, 3-13 thru 3-14

N

National Advisory Committee on
    Microbiological Criteria for
    Foods (*see* government
    regulations and regulatory
    agencies)
National Pest Management
    Association, 11-44
National Restaurant Association,
    1-4, 10-11, 13-19
National Restaurant Association
    Educational Foundation, 13-19
neurotoxic shellfish poisoning
    (NSP), 3-11
NSF International, 4-11, 11-13
NSF International certification mark,
    4-11, 11-13

O

Occupational Safety and Health
    Administration (OSHA) (*see*
    government regulations and
    regulatory agencies)
off-site service, 9-2, 9-12 thru 9-14
    catering, 9-13
    delivery, 9-12 thru 9-13
    vending machine, 9-14
open shelving, 7-6
operating permit (*see* certificate
    of operation)
OSHA (*see* government regulations
    and regulatory agencies)
outdoor dining area, 11-41 thru 11-42
oxygen, 2-6
oyster, 2-15, 2-16